Augsburg College
George Sverdrup Library
Minneapolis, MN 55454

WITHDRAWN

Congressional Television

Recent Titles in Contributions in Political Science
Series Editor: Bernard K. Johnpoll

The Strange Career of Marihuana: Politics and Ideology of Drug Control in America
Jerome L. Himmelstein

French Communism in the Era of Stalin: The Quest for Unity and Integration, 1945–1962
Irwin M. Wall

North Korea in Transition: From Dictatorship to Dynasty
Tai Sung An

The Harmonization of European Public Policy: Regional Responses to Transnational Challenges
Edited by Leon Hurwitz

The Press and the Rebirth of Iberian Democracy
Edited by Kenneth Maxwell

Domestic Policy Formation: Presidential-Congressional Partnership?
Steven A. Shull

Communications Policy and the Political Process
Edited by John J. Havick

Abortion: A Case Study in Law and Morals
Fred M. Frohock

The State as Terrorist: The Dynamics of Governmental Violence and Repression
Edited by Michael Stohl and George A. Lopez

Minority Rights: A Comparative Analysis
Jay A. Sigler

Controlling Regulatory Sprawl: Presidential Strategies from Nixon to Reagan
Howard Ball

Puerto Rican Politics in Urban America
Edited by James Jennings and Monte Rivera

Making Campaigns Count: Leadership and Coalition-Building in 1980
Darrell M. West

Congressional Television

A LEGISLATIVE HISTORY

Ronald Garay

CONTRIBUTIONS IN POLITICAL SCIENCE, NUMBER 111
GREENWOOD PRESS
WESTPORT, CONNECTICUT · LONDON, ENGLAND

Library of Congress Cataloging in Publication Data

Garay, Ronald.
  Congressional television.

  (Contributions in political science, ISSN 0147-1066 ; no. 111)
  Includes bibliographical references and index.
  1. United States. Congress—Television broadcasting of proceedings—History. I. Title. II. Series.
JK1129.G37   1984   328.73′0068   83-18563
ISBN 0-313-23707-7 (lib. bdg.)

Copyright © 1984 by Ronald Garay

All rights reserved. No portion of this book may be reproduced, by any process or technique, without the express written consent of the publisher.

Library of Congress Catalog Card Number: 83-18563
ISBN: 0-313-23707-7
ISSN: 0147-1066

First published in 1984

Greenwood Press
A division of Congressional Information Service, Inc.
88 Post Road West
Westport, Connecticut 06881

Printed in the United States of America

10 9 8 7 6 5 4 3 2 1

To Mom and Dad

Contents

	Preface	ix
1	Factors Influencing House and Senate Television	3
2	Congressional Radio	25
3	Televising Congressional Hearings: Acclaim and Controversy	35
4	Television Covers House Committees and Watergate Investigations	57
5	Congress Considers Chamber Television	85
6	Television Enters the House While the Senate Delays the Inevitable	113
7	The Impact of Congressional Television	131
	Notes	155
	Bibliographical Essay	183
	Index	187

Preface

The inaugural broadcast of America's first radio station, Pittsburgh's KDKA, carried news of the 1920 presidential election returns.[1] From that time forward, broadcasting and politics have been inextricably linked. That relationship and the role it plays in our lives today were characterized in a 1969 congressional report. "[B]roadcasting, and television in particular," reads the report, "has indeed become indispensable to the political processes of our Nation. This has come about, not by virtue of the technological peculiarities of the medium as such, but because the medium—for whatever reason—has become the public's prime source of information."[2]

This book is devoted to one particular aspect of political broadcasting, that of televising the proceedings of the U.S. Senate and the U.S. House of Representatives. Using a format that closely resembles a legislative history,[3] the book traces some sixty years of efforts by individual legislators to implement first radio and then television coverage of congressional hearings, meetings and chamber deliberations.

The book is divided into three parts. Chapter 1 briefly explains how and why television plays such an integral part in the activities of both the collective Congress and individual House and Senate members.

Chapters 2 through 6 comprise the legislative history. These chapters trace the formation and progress of congressional television from its earliest stages into the 1980s. Particular attention is given to issues surrounding televised congressional hearings during the early 1950s and to efforts throughout much of the 1970s to implement televised coverage of House chamber proceedings.

Chapter 7 examines the impact television has had upon member conduct and legislative procedures in the House and Senate and upon the congressional television audience.

For their valuable assistance and encouragement in preparing this book, the author wishes to thank Joseph Berman and John Loos. Thanks also to Laurel Snedden for proofreading and editorial comments. And for her editorial assistance, support and understanding, the author expresses deepest gratitude to his wife, Mary Sue. Finally, appreciation is extended to the U.S. Congress, whose collective membership comprises a sometimes bewildering but always fascinating institution.

Congressional
Television

1 · Factors Influencing House and Senate Television

The United States Congress has been called the "central institution of the American democratic republic"[1] and the "First Branch of Government."[2] Individual members of Congress perform an assortment of tasks, but lawmaking is the constitutionally designated primary "business" of Congress the institution.

In performing its legislative role, Congress must satisfy an American public whose traditional skepticism toward congressional intentions is reflected in a generally low esteem for the institution. Public confidence in Congress has ebbed and flowed over the years, but its erosion during the late 1960s and early 1970s finally reached what was termed a "crisis" stage.[3] A congressionally commissioned study of the situation cited two principal factors for declining public confidence in Congress: 1) the public perception of how Congress conducts its legislative business and 2) the wide cross-section of the public that is misinformed, uninformed or undereducated about congressional matters.[4]

CONGRESSIONAL IMAGE

Polls consistently substantiate the above, as proved in two recent surveys commissioned by Congress. One was conducted in 1977 for the House Commission on Administrative Review (the

House survey).[5] Four years earlier, a similar survey was conducted for the Senate Subcommittee on Intergovernmental Relations (the Senate survey).[6]

The House survey, whose objective was "to evaluate public understanding of the operations of the House and to probe public concerns about the way Members carry out their responsibilities,"[7] asked respondents to rate the performance of the House of Representatives in the past two or three years. Sixty-five percent of the respondents rated congressional performance from "fair" to "poor." When asked to elaborate, some of the more critical comments contended that congressmen were not hardworking, did not do their jobs, bickered and haggled with one another, wasted time, and spent money on the wrong things. The collective Congress was criticized for having done nothing to ease inflation, for not understanding and acting on problems correctly and for implementing poor programs. One of the harshest criticisms was directed toward Congress's inability to cooperate with the President. Of the few positive comments, the most significant was that under the burden of a difficult job Congress appeared to be doing the best it could.[8]

An attitudinal phenomenon appeared when survey respondents were asked to rate the job performance of the U.S. House member representing their own congressional district. Thirteen percent gave their representative an "excellent" rating, 27 percent gave him a "pretty good" rating, and 17 percent gave him an "only fair" rating. Clearly, respondents thought much more of their representative's performance than they did of the congressional performance in general.[9]

Richard Fenno, Jr., in an aptly titled article, "If, as Ralph Nader Says, Congress Is 'The Broken Branch,' How Come We Love Our Congressman So Much?" analyzed the disparity in attitudes toward the individual and the institution and determined that the public applies two sets of standards when judging the activity and accomplishments of the individual and those of Congress the institution. As a result, "Individual legislators are evaluated in terms of personal style and district service . . .," whereas "Congress-as-institution is evaluated largely on the basis of policies—which tend to be intractable and divisive."[10] Fenno also found that, particularly during reelection campaigns, representatives habitually criticize Congress while simultaneously portraying themselves as consistently at odds with the institution. In other words, "Members run *for* Congress by running *against* Congress."[11] Former U.S. Rep. Edward Koch (D-N.Y.) expressed it this way: "When I'm asked about Congress, . . . I say it's doing a lousy job. And if I say that, why shouldn't the constituents around the country say it?"[12]

One additional reason for the low esteem for Congress/high esteem for representative dichotomy is the type of media coverage given each. Network television news tends to ignore individual congressmen (House members more so than senators) and to concentrate on news items that often may be critical of the institutional Congress. Local television stations, on the other hand, rely more heavily on news related to the individual congressman. If a local news item places the congressman in a favorable light, as it often does, it can create a lasting, positive impression among viewers.[13]

The 1973 Senate survey was more inclusive of Congress in general than was the 1977 House survey. Its stated purpose was "to measure public perception of the responsiveness of government at the Federal, State and local levels and to explore ways to increase the responsiveness and efficiency of government at all levels."[14] The survey report concluded with a mixture of pessimism and optimism: "The American people's loss of confidence in their government has reached severe—even majority—proportions today, but, at the same time, the American people and their leaders overwhelmingly believe that government at all levels can work effectively and well."[15]

Congressional Image and Public Information

Attitudes toward Congress are shaped by what the public knows about the institution, and, according to one report, the public knows very little: "[M]ost Americans today have only the most general sense of the constitutional role that Congress performs and few citizens have any clear conception of how Congress carries out its legislative responsibilities."[16]

The problem does not stem from lack of interest in legislative affairs. Indeed, the House survey found that 86 percent of the survey respondents acknowledged some interest in congressional activities.[17] The Senate survey also found a "sizable majority" of respondents indicating that "if sufficiently motivated they would like to respond to government and to the political process."[18] The problem seems rather to lie in the quantity and quality of information reported about Congress. Again, referring to the House survey, thirty-two percent of the respondents said they presently received enough information on congressional activities; but an overwhelming 60 percent said they wanted more information.[19]

The Senate survey showed similar findings. For example, a "substantial majority" of 60 percent of the survey respondents gave themselves a negative rating on "being up-to-date" about what the federal government was doing. Respondents with little education felt least knowledgeable, whereas those with a college education, an income exceeding $15,000, and an interest in community activity, felt best informed—but only by slight margins of difference.[20]

This lack of knowledge may be attributed in part to the American school system. A 1973 citizenship examination administered by the National Assessment of Educational Progress showed that teenagers and young adults "know frighteningly little about the personalities or policies of governmental leaders, and have not even begun to understand the workings of the American political process." And a later report by the National Commission on the Reform of Secondary Education concluded that students are ill-prepared to accept the responsibilities of citizenship due to their failure in comprehending how our political system functions. The National Task Force on Citizenship Education lamented that "neither school nor society presently considers citizenship preparation to be an important function of the schools."[21]

Some blame for Americans' knowledge gap about Congress may also be placed, paradoxically, on television, the primary source of information about government and politics in this country.

Congressional Image and Television

When asked what source they most relied on for information about the government, 65 percent of the Senate survey respondents answered "television news." Newspapers came in second (52 percent) and radio a distant third (39 percent).[22] Television's predominance as a source not only for government news but for all news has been confirmed by another survey conducted by the Roper Organization. The Roper survey also found that television leads all other media in news credibility.[23]

Dependence on and credibility of television news notwithstanding, many persons have criticized both the quantity and the quality of television news reporting. The fact that 60 percent of the House survey respondents and the same percentage of Senate survey respondents felt inadequately informed about congressional matters while nearly the same percentage of respondents relied primarily on television for information is a coincidence that bears a harsh indictment of the medium's reportorial efforts. Criticism also has come from the congressional subjects of the reporting. When asked by the Commission on Administrative Review to list the serious problems of the House regarding its public image, one-third of the House members cited "unfair treatment by the news media."[24]

Addressing itself to the image problem, the Congressional Research Service concluded in 1974:

The times seem appropriate for Congress, as an institution, to look seriously at the process whereby its day to day activities are communicated to the people and to consider ways of improving this process. This goal should be two-fold: 1) to improve the public's knowledge about Congress as it deals with daily problems of concern and 2) to convey a greater sense of the institutional dimension of the legislative process.[25]

TELEVISION AND CONGRESSIONAL PUBLICITY

Congressmen as Self-Publicists

Regardless of the collective feelings of Congress toward the news media, individual congressmen often must rely on local television news both for publicity and for information dissemination. Washington based reporters representing local television stations oblige the congressman's needs by recording interviews with him or by reporting on his legislative activity. Fulfillment of one another's needs—the congressman's need for media attention and the reporter's need for a story—forms a cordial, albeit a symbiotic, relationship between the two.[26]

A problem with the above scenario is that as few as 4 percent of all local television stations maintain Washington based reporters.[27] Since most local broadcasters cannot go to the congressman, the congressman often must supply broadcasters with material prepared by his own staff.

Congressmen may distribute information to television stations in a number of ways. The most common is the printed press release that may be directly incorporated into a newscast or rewritten for the same purpose. A second form is the "actuality," a brief recorded statement by the congressman that may be inserted into a regularly scheduled local newscast. Broadcasters appreciate the actuality because it allows them to employ the actual words and image of the congressman in place of a newsman reading a written account of the statement. A third information form is the periodic "Your Man in Washington" type report. This recorded program differs from the actuality in both length and scope. Lasting anywhere from five minutes to half an hour or more, this program allows a congressman (and sometimes a guest) to discuss a wide range of topics in an informal setting.[28]

As for production facilities and expertise at congressional disposal, the networks could hardly match what is available. Both houses of Congress have their own separate radio-television recording facility. The House Recording Studio, located in the Rayburn House Office Building, is a complex of sound studios, control rooms, tape recorders and high speed duplicating machines—technology which has been described as the "most advanced available."[29] The Senate Recording Studio is located in an abandoned subway tunnel adjoining the Capitol basement. The only dissimilarities in the House and Senate recording facilities are the Senate's fewer studios (four as opposed to six) and smaller staff.[30]

The House "Recording Studio Rate Schedule"[31] provides some idea of services available for the "exclusive use of sitting Members of the House of Representatives":

In addition to the basic recording services, the Studio offers facilities for preparation of teleprompter scripts, transcriptions of recorded material, telephone recordings, post production services on a time-available basis, and television make-up. . . . The Studio offers recommendations for production techniques, formats, sets, and clothing. In general, the Studio will offer Members all possible technical assistance in the production of their programs.[32]

Not all congressmen choose to use the recording studios. In fact, some 20 percent of the House membership claims not to have used them. That figure appears to be decreasing as younger persons enter Congress. Interviews with U.S. Representatives who first entered Congress in 1958, 1968 or 1978 revealed that new members overwhelmed the old in their reliance on the studios. According to Michael J. Robinson, the 1978 class "was more than three times as likely as the oldest to have used the recording studios once a week or more."[33]

Television News and Congressional Publicity

Congressmen cannot rely entirely on their individually produced television programs for publicity. They must also rely on news media representatives of the Capitol Hill press corps. Press releases and personal interviews are the primary means by which congressmen make contact with reporters.[34] Congressional offices are noteworthy as sources of prolific numbers of press releases, but the opportunity to be interviewed obviously surpasses that of handing out a mimeographed piece of paper.[35]

The television reporter theoretically shares the same access to members of Congress as do his print media colleagues. Realistically, the television reporter's access is restricted because of the press facilities available to him, the ground rules under which he must work, and the problems imposed by television's time limitations and visual needs.

Since the late 1940s, radio and television reporters have occupied their own press galleries in the vicinity of both congressional chambers.[36] The radio and television galleries are supervised by the Executive Committee of the Radio and Television Correspondents' Galleries, but admittance to them must be approved by either the Senate Rules and Administration Committee or the Speaker of the House. In 1981, the combined membership of the House and Senate radio and television galleries numbered just over one thousand. Membership ranged from reporters representing all the national network news organizations to those representing television and radio stations in remote and sparsely populated locales.[37]

Few restraints are placed on the television reporter's coverage of Congress as long as he limits himself to observation and note-taking, but when he wishes to use cameras to record or televise a congressional event or interview, he is hampered by restrictions. Reporters must follow explicit instructions on where, when and in what manner they may cover House and Senate activity whenever such coverage occurs in the vicinity of the Capitol Building and the House and Senate office buildings.[38]

The problems posed by having to work around these restrictions are formidable but perhaps not so formidable as problems posed by working conditions in the radio and television galleries. These problems relate primarily to space. In the Senate radio-television gallery, where the problem is most acute, television reporters must work alongside radio reporters and technical personnel in the same space originally provided for radio alone in 1945.[39] The gallery houses only one small studio that may be utilized for television interviewing. In contrast, the House radio-television gallery is almost twice the size of the Senate's and contains one large studio and three smaller ones, all of which can be used for either radio or television interviewing.[40]

All who work in the Senate gallery—reporters and production crews from all the national radio and television network news organizations, non-network news services such as United Press International (UPI) Audio, regional network or broadcast group organizations such as Westinghouse and individual radio and television stations—must share working space to the extent that some persons must periodically vacate the facilities in order to allow others room to work.[41]

Two additional problems encountered by television reporters are the enormity of the area that must be covered while searching for news and the questionable expertise which some reporters bring to their job. In reference to the first point, an "average day" on Capitol Hill usually means that "a television network will be represented by one or two correspondents, a field producer and at least one three-man camera crew,"[42] responsible for covering the activity of "535 members [of Congress] and hundreds of standing committees, subcommittees, and joint committees spread out over a ten-square-block area."[43]

Given the ground that must be covered, there nonetheless are few television reporters designated as congressional correspondents who actually devote full time to covering Congress. Robert O. Blanchard found that well over half of the network congressional reporters he surveyed spent less than 60 percent of their time covering Congress.[44] Congressional reporters from broadcast groups and local stations spent more time covering Congress, but it may be surmised that reporters in both categories were concentrating more on individual congressmen (for the "local angle") than the institutional Congress on which the networks focus.[45]

Returning to problems of reporting, the logistics dilemma is compounded by poor preparation and meager training on the part of many reporters given the chore of having to understand not only highly technical congressional procedures but also complex issues of an infinite variety. Lee M. Mitchell has charged that, as a result, television reporters resort to "herd journalism"[46] in which some reporters rely on others to set the agenda for what will be covered. This means that the most interesting and most visual topics and individuals normally get the most attention. And for Congress, the attention attracted by the Senate generally has been disproportionate to that attracted by the House.

Television Concentration on the Senate

The U.S. House of Representatives has been referred to as the chamber "where the public's business is performed,"[47] as the "co-equal branch of government closest to the people,"[48] and as "the most public of our institutions—*the place of access*, of contact with the people."[49] All of this may be true, but the limelight of public attention has been taken by the U.S. Senate in recent years. Some have traced the departure of public awareness from the House to the failure of the press (print and electronic) in covering its activities,[50] while others have traced the rise in public awareness of the Senate to the television attention it has received.[51]

One of the keys to the Senate's predominance is the part many of its members play in presidential politics. Although one study, referring to the Senate as a "presidential incubator," found that senators were influential as presidential contenders prior to the age of television,[52] there has been an overwhelming number of contenders coming from the senatorial ranks since 1960. One ingredient in a senator's rise to prominence is his ability to create news and to make himself a national celebrity.[53] He nurtures media attention, and the media, especially network television, accommodate his overtures.

Several studies support the contention that the Senate dominates congressional-related television news. The Blanchard study cited above found that only 9 percent of the network reporters interviewed spent most of their time covering the House, while 64 percent spent most of their time covering the Senate.[54] A 1976 study by Michael J. Robinson and Kevin Appel showed that of the network news stories related to Congress (a substantial 15 percent of the total number of stories aired on all three commercial networks), those focusing on the Senate outnumbered those focusing on the House by a five-to-three ratio. The ratio dropped to four to three when time or news seconds alone was used as a base of comparison. Robinson and Appel also found no difference among the three national commercial networks in their proclivity for Senate over House stories.[55]

A study of congressional appearances on network television interview programs provides yet another example of the Senate's predominance. William C. Adams and Paul H. Ferber examined the guest lists of "Meet the Press," "Face the Nation," and "Issues and Answers" that aired from 1965 through 1974 and concluded that "no other group of office-holders even approach the visibility which Senators are granted on these programs." Senators were featured guests on at least one-fourth of the programs and received four times the amount of television exposure received by House members.[56]

The media attention devoted to the Senate contrasted with that devoted to the House led one observer to say that "the increasing irrelevance of the House in American life is attributable at least in some proportion to the degree to which its activities and people remain a mystery to the public."[57]

Television Coverage of Congressional Committees

There are only two institutional activities of Congress that both houses have opened to television cameras—congressional hearings and meetings. Though television access is a reality, it is not complete. The movement to open more committees to "let the sunshine in" has been a difficult and lengthy task.[58] The issue of television in the committee rooms has caused, in many instances, the more secrecy-prone veterans of Congress to clash with younger members who favor greater public access. And yet, there have been those, even among the veterans, who have seized upon the television coverage to turn certain committee activities into media events.

During committee deliberations, hearings may be called to allow spokesmen with certain points of view or with particular information to present testimony to the committee. "Ideally," says Nelson W. Polsby, "[hearings] are an effective research device—a way of focusing the attention of congressmen on the substantive merits of a proposed bill and its possible pitfalls."[59]

Hearings are not always conducted just to consider matters related to pending legislation. "Sometimes committee chairmen will ask that hearings be organized simply to furnish general information to the members or in order to investigate the execution of laws by an executive department."[60] The 1950s Kefauver Crime Committee hearings were an example of hearings conducted for informational purposes. The other purpose of the investigatory hearing is exemplified by oversight hearings where representatives of agencies such as the Federal Communications Commission are questioned about their performance.

Douglas Cater has charged that "committee investigations are seldom in point of fact 'investigations.' They are planned deliberately to move from a preconceived idea to a predetermined conclusion. . . . The hearing is the final act in the drama."[61] Others have concluded that investigative hearings have been orchestrated to produce publicity—publicity directed toward individuals as well as issues.[62] Lawrence Leamer, for example, described the sudden appearance of several prominent senators during Senate Constitutional Rights Subcommittee hearings to question witness Walter Cronkite just as television news film cameras began to roll. When Cronkite's testimony ended, the filming ceased, and the senators who had arrived only shortly before disappeared. Other witnesses remained, but the Senate panel left to question them was almost depleted once the cameras were turned off.[63]

Such abuse of purpose is apparent at times, but when television news cameras are present, committee investigations do provide Congress with a legitimate national platform to counter the considerable coverage given views emanating from the White House.[64] This method of sparring with the executive branch was for many years the only means available for the institutional Congress to appeal for public support on proposed legislation.[65]

Taking advantage of television's presence is often a matter of "catch-when-catch-can," since congressional committees are not guaranteed coverage. Moreover, when television crews do appear, they usually cover only a brief portion of the entire hearing. This was not the case during the 1950s and 1960s, when television networks would occasionally preempt scheduled programming to air extended hearing coverage. The networks later curtailed that practice, only to return to it momentarily during the Watergate years.[66] Apart from Watergate, only those congressional hearings whose subjects were "extraordinarily dramatic" were granted extended network television coverage during the 1970s.[67]

The pressure of network economics has been a prime factor affecting the amount of congressional committee coverage. Since loss of regular programs amounts to loss in revenue, network executives have been less willing to allow news departments to preempt the programs. The business managers of commercial television have even conditioned news personnel to request less time to air committee activity. Financial demands have restricted public television less than commercial television, but the expense of extended coverage has limited even what the Public Broadcasting Service (PBS) can provide.[68]

Although issues of extreme public interest are the only ones to attract extended coverage, numerous items related to congressional committees are often reported on network news programs. One study found that "the most frequent type of congressional coverage involves 'committee action' of one sort or another—committee reports, committee votes, and, above all, committee hearings." The study also revealed that reports on committee activity tended to be longer than reports on other congressional activity.[69]

Committees oftentimes must compete with one another for television coverage due to the simultaneous scheduling of their meetings. As an example, Lee M. Mitchell cited a randomly selected day in April 1974 when forty-seven committee meetings were scheduled within a six and one-half hour period. Even when a congressional committee is covered, the film or tape of what may have been a lengthy session must be edited to fit a program slot of only a few minutes' (or seconds') duration—that is, if the news producer feels the committee segment is newsworthy (or *more* newsworthy than other items with which the committee story could be replaced) and has the necessary visual qualities of a network newscast.[70]

TELEVISION AND THE PRESIDENT

For much of this century, policy-making issues confronting our national government typically were resolved by what appeared to be executive initiative. It was acknowledged that presidential energy, skill and force were the sole ingredients necessary for a unified government. Such presidential aggrandizement led to what has been termed the "cult of the strong Presidency." The President was not content just to manage the executive branch; he also "became the acknowledged leader of the legislative branch." In effect, the President set the congressional agenda.[71]

The fact that the President had become the "Chief Legislator," whose policy program was "institutionalized as a point of departure for the legislative process," did not inspire great public confidence in the ability of Congress to ascend to a leadership role of any significance. In fact, a noticeable dilution of congressional power was more the result of presidential domination. Political scientists voiced several reasons for the congressional decline. One was the emergence of matters related to military and foreign affairs following World War II: "Presidential initiative in these areas is enunciated in the Constitution and validated by historical experience; and, since these international and military concerns are enhanced by current events, the President and the executive establishment are in turn enhanced."[72]

A second reason for congressional decline has been the inability of Congress to compete with presidential publicity. Since the complexity and the interdependency of the two governmental branches have made their exercise of power less distinct from one another,

> the dynamic power of each branch is more or less determined by its ability to communicate *directly* with the electorate, so as to justify and gain the confidence of the public for their respective actions. According to this view, communication *itself* is power, and exclusive access to the communication media is an unchecked, unbalanced power. If one branch of the government is able to gain nearly exclusive or at least effective access to any or all of the media, while the other branches are more or less excluded, the balance of power will lean in the direction of the branch with access.[73]

The power and the prestige of the presidency have been enhanced by a virtually unencumbered access to the nation's broadcast media. In the words of Judge J. Skelly Wright,

> Television has become, in recent years, a principal vehicle by which the President presents to the public his views on important issues of the day. Indeed, no single fact of our changing political life overrides the significance of the expansion of the President's ability to obtain immediate and direct access to the people through the communications media.[74]

Presidential Access to Television

The President obviously has no constitutional authority to usurp the powers of Congress, but his influence over the direction Congress takes on many pieces of legislation has been derived indirectly by his public support and, in turn, by public support

Factors Influencing House and Senate Television 17

of his views on legislation.[75] When a president "goes to the people," he tries to "focus the attention of the mass media . . . on an issue" and to "communicate his concern about the issue. He can increase its general visibility, stir up interest-group activity, and, to a certain extent, set the terms in which it will be debated."[76] And, as one commentator said, "[A]nyone who can set the terms of a debate can win it."[77]

The current ease with which the President gains television access is due in equal parts to the natural interest the public shows in news of his activity and the need for the news media in general to offer their audience something that will attract and sustain attention. News about the President "combines governmental information with human interest. He is both a public institution and a person, with foibles, weaknesses, human involvements, and the rest, as well as policy positions and philosophies."[78] And when television news focuses on any one of these aspects, as it often does, the President's "inflated currency of publicity" flourishes.[79]

The President uses a number of television formats, all directed to publicizing either his activities or his views on particular issues. He may call a press conference, make a formal address to the nation, consent to an interview, receive visiting heads of state, or take a trip to other parts of this country or abroad.[80] A common strand among all these is the control the President exerts in deciding how, when and where television will be allowed to cover him. Since all three commercial television networks have a policy of presidential coverage whenever possible, it is an easy matter for the White House to dictate the ground rules.[81]

One example of White House control is the presidential press conference—an event that blends careful staging with fragments of spontaneity. The President is cued by a broadcast representative when to enter the conference room in order that the proceedings may begin on the hour or half hour. The President usually opens with one or two announcements and then responds to questions from reporters. The subject matter of most questions is obvious, the President's answers typically well rehearsed. Once the President has expressed his views, the press conference ends. All is usually conducted within a half hour in deference to the program schedule of the broadcast networks.[82]

The televised press conference provides the President not only a forum to impart information and opinion but also a pulpit from which to express partisan political views. During a 1976 hearing before the House Communications Subcommittee, Rep. Torbert MacDonald (D-Mass.) questioned the propriety of such a practice in reference to an incident involving President Ford and one of his opponents in the 1976 presidential primary campaigns:

> One week before the New Hampshire primary President Ford called a news conference at the White House "to announce his plans for reorganizing the U.S. intelligence operations." . . . On at least two occasions during that half-hour conference President Ford delivered extended political attacks on his opponent Ronald Reagan and the very next day the Washington Star quoted a White House aide as saying that Mr. Ford had carefully prepared his remarks on Reagan and intended to deliver them regardless of the specific thrust of any question he was asked about the primary.[83]

A year earlier, not only President Ford's remarks but his appearance alone would have obligated the television networks airing his press conference to offer equal time for a response by candidate Reagan under the "equal opportunity" provisions of the Communications Act.[84] But President Ford was the beneficiary of a 1975 Federal Communications Commission ruling that exempted presidential press conferences from the equal opportunity requirements.[85] Congress had amended the Communications Act in 1959 to exempt broadcasters from equal opportunity obligations whenever announced candidates for public office appeared in a "bona fide newscast," "bona fide news interview," "bona fide news documentary," and "on-the-spot coverage of bona fide news events."[86] However, a 1964 ruling by the FCC declared that presidential press conferences did not fall into any of the exemption categories.[87] The 1975 ruling reversed the FCC's 1964 ruling and thus granted an additional prerogative for presidents thereafter to say whatever they pleased during a press conference.

The most effective presidential television format is the formal address. The address usually pertains to an important event or policy decision for which the President has requested simultaneous program time on all national television (and radio) networks during prime time—when the viewing audience is at its peak.

The formal presidential television address . . . is a powerful instrument. With as much or as little time as he chooses, with control over format and visual techniques, with the built-in audience for prime-time entertainment, and unimpeded by questions, the president can carefully develop and argue for a policy decision. He can thus present a complex or controversial position effectively, perhaps uniting a divided citizenry on an international issue, creating public support for a legislative initiative, or simply avoiding the necessity of having his views questioned by a skeptical press.[88]

A 1976 Congressional Research Service (CRS) study showed that during the decade from 1966 to 1976 practically every request for simultaneous time to air a presidential address was granted by NBC, CBS and ABC. Two bases for the routine practice were outlined by network spokesmen:

first, a presumption by the networks that any given Presidential address prepared solely for television almost surely will prove to be sufficiently newsworthy to justify preemption of regular network programming; second, a complementary premise that a Presidential address, regardless of its substance, has a unique inherent news value because of the importance of the Presidential office.[89]

The CRS study concluded, "These premises appear presumptively to commit the networks to coverage of Presidential addresses and virtually to entrust the President with judging their news value."[90]

An October 1974 event illustrates the presidential power to obtain network television time. President Ford was scheduled to deliver an address on the nation's economy to a meeting of the Future Farmers of America in Kansas City. The White House informed the three commercial television networks that the speech would be delivered and that television coverage would be allowed. All three networks declined to accept the coverage invitation until the White House made a formal request that the President be covered. As soon as the request was made, all three networks reversed themselves and agreed to make air time available. When William Sheehan, President of ABC News, was later asked about the coverage decision, he replied, "Historically, any time a President flat-out asks for air-time, he gets it . . . when the President wants to speak to the nation, there's no way we can deny him the air."[91] A similar but earthier remark once was made by former NBC President Julian Goodman when asked to explain the network's attitude toward President Nixon's numerous television appearances. "Our attitude," said Goodman, "is the same as our attitude toward previous Presidents: he can have any goddamn thing he wants."[92]

REFORM

This chapter thus far has examined problems encountered by Congress regarding its public image, its public support and its ability to inform and educate the public as to its composition, procedures and legislative role. Evidence has been presented illustrating the inability of Congress, especially the House of Representatives, to attract the kind of publicity afforded the President by the national television networks. The presidential-congressional struggle for publicity has been central to the legislative history of congressional television. But the origins of this inter-branch struggle are much more expansive than might be explained by a mere conflict over publicity. The struggle is rooted in what has been perceived, either rightly or wrongly, as an erosion of congressional prerogatives that tipped the executive-legislative balance of power towards the President. The decision to improve accessibility to television, while a direct result of congressional efforts to modernize many of its antiquated rules and procedures, nonetheless appeared to coincide with Congress's efforts to reestablish its policy-making initiative.

Resurgence of Congressional Policy-Making

The Joint Committee on the Organization of Congress stated the following in a 1966 report:

Many contend that Congress no longer is capable of exercising initiative in the solution of modern problems. A fundamental reason for this loss of initiative is the lack of organizational effectiveness. Under the pressure of modern circumstances, the Congress has tended to delegate authority to the executive branch of the government. While Congress has not abdicated its role, it has permitted that role to become diluted.[93]

What is noteworthy about the statement is that it came at a time when Congress was beginning a self-evaluation of its relationship with the President. That evaluation occupied what James L. Sundquist has called "a remarkable period of congressional introspection—surely the most intense such period, perhaps the only one, in the history of that institution."[94] As a result, Congress would become a more assertive body, assertive in the sense that it would revitalize its legal authority "to participate in policy making—especially in the areas of declaration and termination of national emergencies, war-making, foreign policy, intelligence operations, budget policy, and impoundments of appropriated funds."[95]

The determination to reassert congressional powers has been attributed to at least three factors occurring in the last decade: the prolonged U.S. involvement in Vietnam, the Watergate scandal of the Nixon administration and a change in congressional membership.[96] A fourth factor has been the nature of the congressional-presidential relationship. Some political scientists suggest that presidents have occasionally appeared who perhaps more than some of their predecessors have regarded their office as a place of supreme power. These chief executives have been able to convince Congress to delegate certain authority to them, although the authority had been constitutionally mandated to Congress. Delegation of this kind has been likened to Congress tossing "power over a barrier . . . into alien territory—out of direct control, out of easy reach, even out of sight." At some point, says Sundquist, "the urge arises in Congress to take back its power."[97]

Some political scientists contend that the exchange of power between the President and Congress has appeared with consistency throughout the nineteenth and twentieth centuries. The components of this "cyclical theory" have been described as beginning with a Congress that, due to problems of leadership, coordination and oversight, "decentralized itself out of the quest for power by its members." During the quest to reassert its authority, Congress engages in moments of intense introspection. Its constitutional role is reassessed, and a determination is made to reform its ways.[98]

Congressional reform movements have resulted from several factors, only one of which has been the external influence of increasing presidential power. Two internal influences have been "the continually shifting distribution of power within Congress" and the "recurring efforts to guarantee that Congress properly represents the nation and fulfills its responsibilities."[99] These factors have led to at least three significant reform periods in the last half century.

The first occurred in the 1940s and led to passage of the 1946 Legislative Reorganization Act.[100] Another reform period gained prominence in the 1960s and resulted in passage of the Legislative Reorganization Act of 1970. Most of the Act's provisions pertained to floor and committee procedures in both congressional houses. In particular, open hearings and committee business meetings were encouraged, and broadcast coverage of hearings was to be permitted in the House, as it already was in the Senate.[101]

The open meeting suggestions of the 1970 Act were slow to take hold in either house. But as criticism mounted over the extent of public business being conducted in secrecy, Congress was persuaded to open more of its committee sessions to the public. The House was the first to adopt the so-called sunshine rules in 1973, opening all committee meetings (including "mark-up" sessions where final drafts of bills are hammered into shape) unless a majority of the committee voted to close its doors by calling an executive session. The Senate adopted similar rules in 1975. House and Senate conference committee meetings were also opened to the public in 1975.[102] Television benefitted from the move toward committee openness, since public access usually meant television access as well.

The reforms of the 1946 and 1970 Legislative Reorganization Acts were basically structural, motivated more by internal congressional forces than by external forces. Congressional reforms of the mid–1970s, though, resulted from a combination of the two. Externally, Vietnam and Watergate led the list of incentives to reform. Legislative measures related to these two issues began flowing as the Ninety-third Congress convened in 1973. In fact, Bruce R. Hopkins stated that "[f]or those who watch Congress and seek consequence in the ebbs and flows of relations between the legislative and executive branches, 1973 was an incomparable year." And he continued, "During its first session the Ninety-third Congress attempted more—many more—ways to reform and strengthen itself as an institution than nearly any previous Congress."[103]

Internally, reforms grew from an extraordinary change in the complexion of congressional membership. The Watergate scandal that had eroded public confidence in the President also eroded public confidence in Congress. As a result, "a huge class of freshmen stormed Washington" to convene the Ninety-fourth Congress in 1975. The House freshman class was the largest since 1949 and represented twenty-six percent of the House Democrats and twelve percent of the House Republicans. Furthermore, most of the new members "represented the first large infusion of the '1960s awareness' into the House." Many had campaigned for and were dedicated to achieving reform.[104]

By 1975, the House of Representatives had outdistanced the Senate in revising its organizational procedures. It had changed the method for selecting committee chairmen so that longevity of service would no longer give senior House members automatic ascendance into powerful committee positions. Newly elected House members were given power that previously had been reserved for more senior members.[105] And the House had taken the lead in opening its committee meetings to the public.

Reform efforts flowing from the 1970 Legislative Reorganization Act gained momentum that would lead Congress to seriously consider opening its legislative chambers to live television coverage. The efforts of chamber television advocates, aided primarily by the activity of the Joint Committee on Congressional Operations, were rewarded in 1979 when telecasts of House deliberative chamber proceedings became a reality.

2 · Congressional Radio

The first U.S. radio broadcasting service had begun by the end of 1920,[1] and by May 1922, statistics showed that 218 radio stations located in most of the U.S. population centers were broadcasting programs ranging from market and weather reports to concerts and lectures.[2] The country was "afire with radio fever"[3] with listeners tuning in on their store-bought or home-built receivers (whose numbers ranged between an estimated 1.5 to 2.5 million)[4] to hear anything the broadcasters could manage to air.

Radio's potential for serving the U.S. Congress as a public information medium was obvious; moreover, broadcasting U.S. House and Senate proceedings directly from their respective chambers was just the sort of novelty programming listeners were likely to find attractive. Several congressmen were intrigued by the idea and were willing either to introduce legislation or to lend their support toward implementing some form of congressional radio.

LEGISLATIVE EFFORTS TO IMPLEMENT CONGRESSIONAL RADIO

The first legislative measure related to radio coverage of congressional activity was introduced by Rep. Vincent Brennan (R-Mich.) in February 1922. The resolution (H.J.Res. 278), providing for the "installation and operation of radiotelephone transmitting apparatus for the purpose of transmitting the proceedings and debates of the Senate and the House of Representatives,"[5] failed to win committee approval. Undaunted, Sen. Robert Howell (R-Nebr.) introduced a more ambitious resolution (S.Res. 197) two years later directing the Secretary of War and the Secretary of the Navy to appoint a joint commission of radio experts from their two departments to investigate and report on "equipment necessary for the broadcasting by radio of the proceedings of the Senate and the House . . . throughout the country, utilizing the radio stations of the War and Navy Departments."[6]

Senator Howell's choice of the War and Navy Departments to conduct the radio investigation derived from the considerable years of experience both had had in apparatus design and transmission research. The Navy especially had been entrusted with the administration of the entire U.S. wireless communications industry during and shortly after World War I. At the same time it had developed a network of powerful coastal radio stations used primarily for transmitting messages to ships.[7] One of these stations near Washington had been used in December 1922, to actually originate President Warren G. Harding's address to Congress from the House chamber. The speech was relayed from the Washington station to numerous other stations and was heard throughout much of the nation.[8]

Owners of private radio stations were quick to grasp the public service potential of broadcasting not just presidential addresses but congressional debate. General James G. Harbord, President of the Radio Corporation of America, had vowed during the May 15, 1923, dedication of RCA's station WJZ in New York City that the station would "gather from . . . all available sources all that will instruct and entertain, and hurl it over millions of square miles of territory."[9] And on the morning of March 28, 1924, just prior to Senator Howell's formal remarks introducing S.Res. 197, RCA representatives had met with him to offer free time on their station to broadcast the proceedings of Congress.[10]

The Howell resolution was referred to the Senate Rules Committee where it was amended slightly and then reported favorably to the full Senate. The Senate approved S.Res. 197 on May 2, 1924.[11]

More than three years passed before a War and Navy Department report was submitted, but when it finally arrived its findings effectively squelched congressional radio for the present. If the Senate had chosen to proceed with the idea, the Army and Navy would have had to reoutfit their radio transmission facilities with new equipment, rent telephone lines to relay the radio signal from point to point and broadcast on frequencies reserved for commercial broadcasters. The latter would have required special congressional dispensation to accomplish and would not have pleased the broadcasting industry. The former would have cost in excess of three million dollars with annual maintenance costs estimated in excess of one million dollars.[12] Congressional radio would have to wait.

The efforts of persons both inside and outside of Congress to implement some form of congressional radio had evolved from a genuine interest in the medium. Senator Howell, for example, was noted in the amateur radio publication *Radio Broadcast* as "one of the very earliest radio zealots in America," having acquired his scientific bent as a graduate of the U.S. Naval Academy and later having traveled to Europe to study radio's municipal uses.[13] The editor of *Radio Broadcast* was fervent in his advocacy of congressional radio. At one time he admonished Congress not to fall behind the British Parliament which, in early 1925, was considering broadcasting its debates.[14] On another occasion he warned that Congress soon would be "forced to broadcast its activities" as a means of keeping pace with increasing presidential use of radio.[15] How effectively the President used and would continue to use radio was underscored by a *New York Times* comment following a 1923 radio address by Calvin Coolidge: "The voice of the people will probably be responsive as never before to the voice to the people, for that voice has literally as never before the ear of the people."[16]

Members of Congress withdrew their attention to congressional radio for the moment, even though legislative bodies elsewhere were showing increased interest in the subject. The British House of Commons, as noted above, had considered some form of parliamentary radio in 1926 but had rejected the idea.

During the same period, the parliaments of Finland, Germany and Japan had begun experimenting with radio coverage of parliamentary proceedings. [17]

Congressional radio was not completely abandoned in the U.S. Congress. Sen. Clarence Dill (D-Wash.) introduced measures during each of the successive first sessions of the Seventieth through the Seventy-third Congress (1928–1933) calling for equipping individual Senate desks with microphones and switching devices to allow for broadcasts from the Senate chamber. [18] Senator Howell introduced an additional measure in 1931 (S.Res. 28) asking only that a select committee be appointed to "investigate the practicability of broadcasting proceedings of the . . . Senate." [19] Sen. Key Pittman (D-Nev.) introduced a similar measure (S.Res. 93) in 1937. His resolution called for an investigation by the Senate Commerce Committee and apparently was prompted by the senator's desire to have some method to circumvent what he considered misleading print media accounts of Senate activity.[20] None of these resolutions generated much interest, and none ever was reported from committee.

Sen. Gerald Nye (R-N.Dak.), although making no formal proposal, did suggest in 1929 that a federal radio station, operating at fifty thousand watts of power, be erected in Washington, D.C., for the purpose of "broadcasting important debates in Congress, for addresses by Federal department executives, for the use of government departments and for the use of all political parties during campaigns."[21] Had such a station been built, its physical characteristics would have drastically limited its listenership. In the first place, a station transmitting at fifty thousand watts would cover only about half the country—and only at night. In the second place, atmospheric conditions would limit the station's coverage area to about 250 miles during the daytime hours when Congress normally would be conducting its business.

INTEREST IN CONGRESSIONAL RADIO: NOVELTY VERSUS NEED

What Congress refused to provide by law, broadcasters determined to acquire by stealth. As the time neared for a House vote to repeal the Eighteenth Amendment in December 1932, representatives of two radio networks (presumably the National Broadcasting Corporation [NBC] and the Columbia Broadcasting System [CBS]) approached House Speaker John Nance Garner (D-Tex.) to ask his permission to broadcast the event. Garner refused. The determined broadcasters then arranged to place microphones in the doorway of a library adjoining the House chamber and to boost the microphone's volume high enough to catch the floor debate and votes. The coverage was a success. In fact, "So favorable were the comments and so high the public interest in the repeal vote," stated the *New York Times*, "that the broadcasters have taken a new hope that before long radio will invade Congress just as it has almost every other realm where people speak or sing."[22]

The absence of Senate and House debate on the matter has concealed the membership's attitudes toward congressional radio. It might be assumed that most congressmen would have objected to placing their institution's activity among the other curiosity pieces then flooding the airwaves. But there were more fundamental issues to be resolved—issues that might be presumed to have been debated in private if not in public. Did, for instance, radio have a legitimate role in the legislative forum? If so, what should that role be? How would broadcasts of congressional proceedings affect the institution? How would they affect the individual members? And who ultimately would control such broadcasts, Congress or broadcasters? These questions would continue unanswered far into the approaching television age.

Those few congressmen who attempted to interest their colleagues in broadcasting congressional proceedings might have been more successful had the national radio networks not been so generous in allowing individual congressmen access to the airwaves. One network, NBC, had a policy throughout the 1930s of allowing free time to any member of Congress requesting it.[23] A similar policy at CBS allowed broadcast on that network of some seven hundred speeches by U.S. Senators and five hundred by U.S. Representatives between 1928 and 1940.[24] With such individual ease of access to the network airwaves, the need for institutional access was significantly diminished.

Nonetheless, advocates of congressional radio continued

steadfastly to press for their cause. During the early-to-mid–1940s, advocacy was particularly strong among several labor unions and professional organizations working outside the halls of Congress. The Congress of Industrial Organizations, the American Federation of Labor, the Writers War Board, the National Planning Association, the Union for Democratic Action and others endorsed proposals for broadcasting congressional proceedings.[25] World War II was in no small measure responsible for stimulating interest in the subject. Maintenance of a strong democracy, stated the representative of one of the above organizations, was the function of an informed American public, information that resulted from direct access via radio to congressional proceedings. Implicit in some of the proposals suggested by these groups was criticism of newspapers for failing to properly inform their readers of congressional activity, especially activity occurring during the war which so dramatically affected everyone.[26]

Individual citizens were also lending substantial support to congressional broadcasting. A 1946 poll found that 51 percent of the public favored construction of a Washington, D.C., radio station to broadcast congressional debates. Only 42 percent, however, were willing to pay additional taxes to finance the station's construction.[27]

A nationwide survey of radio executives found a similar receptiveness to congressional broadcasting. Of the 133 executives questioned, nearly 70 percent favored putting Congress on the air.[28]

CONGRESSIONAL IMPLEMENTATION EFFORTS REVIVED

Outside interest in congressional broadcasting revived interest in the subject among several congressmen. On August 15, 1944, Sen. Claude Pepper (D-Fla.) introduced S.J.Res. 145,[29] to be followed one month later by the introduction of an identical resolution (H.J.Res. 311) in the House by Rep. John Coffee (D-Wash.). The measures noted that the "mounting public interest throughout the country" in congressional activity, particularly as Congress began debating the major social, economic and political issues that would affect the postwar United States, should make it imperative that House and Senate proceedings be broadcast. As Senator Pittman had done in 1937, the Pepper-Coffee resolutions suggested that congressional broadcasts would provide a direct voice to the public, thus circumventing the print media's sometimes misleading reports of congressional activity. The resolutions' implementation provisions authorized the Architect of the Capitol to arrange for facilities to broadcast floor proceedings live and to record proceedings for later distribution. Any radio station or network wanting to carry the proceedings would be free to do so.

The failure of the Pepper-Coffee resolutions to clear committee surprised no one. Remarking on the reluctance of his colleagues to air Senate and House sessions, Pepper said, "If we don't broadcast the proceedings some time and keep step with the advance of radio, the people are going to begin asking whether we are afraid to let them hear what we are saying. It's their business we are transacting."[30]

On January 8, 1947, Senator Pepper introduced a new version of his congressional broadcast measure, this time as S.J.Res. 16.[31] One major provision change would have allowed for broadcast of committee proceedings as well as Senate and House chamber proceedings. The resolution suffered the same fate as its predecessors, dying in committee.

Senator Pepper remained a staunch supporter of congressional broadcasting, nurturing the idea through three more decades while he himself moved from the Senate to the House. Before making his move, Senator Pepper did achieve success of sorts by helping to initiate the first serious discussion of congressional broadcasting in a congressional forum—during hearings conducted by the Joint Committee on the Organization of Congress.

The joint committee—better known as the LaFollette-Monroney Committee for its co-chairmen, Sen. Robert M. LaFollette, Jr. (Prog-Wis.) and Rep. Mike Monroney (D-Okla.)—conducted hearings from March through June 1945. The committee's purpose was to explore new methods and machinery for improving and strengthening the legislative process. Rep. Everett Dirksen (R-Ill.) characterized the committee's formation as a response to the congressional need "to revamp our techniques, to examine this structure in which we work, to modernize it, to make it a branch of Government which operates with speed and dispatch, to make it fulfill not only every responsibility which the Constitution imposes upon it, [but also] to make it function as the people expect."[32]

Several committee witnesses commented on congressional broadcasting. Most favored some form of radio coverage but warned of problems that would have to be overcome. How, for instance, would listeners react to the routine, technical and oftentimes boring congressional debate? How would Congress deter demagoguery and the desire of some congressmen to speak on any subject for any length of time just to get the ear of their constituents? And what about those congressmen who had expert legislative abilities and distinguished records but whose chamber speaking left much to be desired: would voters unfairly penalize them for their poor radio performance? Also cited was the physical problem of simultaneously broadcasting the individual floor proceedings with both houses of Congress in session at the same time.

How could these and similar problems be resolved? One witness suggested that certain times be set aside during regular deliberations in the House and Senate chambers so that congressmen, under agreed-upon time limits, could broadcast their views on key matters.[33] Others suggested that special periods be scheduled, perhaps some at night and all well publicized in advance, for broadcasting congressional debates with all sides being given equal time.[34] Rep. Estes Kefauver (D-Tenn.) felt that floor debate on topics of great interest should be broadcast verbatim. Senator Pepper agreed and added that radio would be especially effective in airing congressional hearings of public interest. Both Kefauver and Pepper stated that once the public got a taste of selected congressional proceedings, it would demand that more be broadcast.[35] As for the problem of simultaneously broadcasting proceedings in both congressional houses, one suggested solution was that two frequencies (presumably clear channels) be reserved—one for each house—with selected committee meetings broadcast during the afternoon.[36]

Representative Coffee, commenting on public judgments of congressmen who might fare poorly as radio performers, said,

"A man does not have to make speeches necessarily to call to the attention of the public that he is their representative." Coffee felt that as long as those who said little were nonetheless sincere in what they said, their listening constituents could readily discern that sincerity and would be properly appreciative.[37]

The work of the LaFollette-Monroney Committee concluded in passage of the Legislative Reorganization Act of 1946.[38] Although the committee recommended that a number of reform provisions for modernizing Congress be included in the law, congressional broadcasting was not one of them. Robert E. Summers later characterized the committee's omission as one of benign neglect:

> None of the witnesses appearing before the Committee in 1945 presented a clear-cut program of action or indicated any specific benefits to be gained through broadcasting the proceedings of Congress. There was no serious consideration of the content of such broadcasts, nor any evidence presented that Congressional proceedings would constitute good radio program fare. The testimony was characterized by a lack of definition, by an air of vague indecision.[39]

CONGRESSIONAL TELEVISION IN ASCENDANCE

Shortly after passage of the 1946 Legislative Reorganization Act, radio, for all practical purposes, had been removed from consideration as a congressional broadcasting medium. Television would soon replace radio as the more popular of the two media, as witnessed by the late 1940s' surge in the manufacture and purchase of television receivers. A corresponding surge in television station construction, program development, and advertiser interest focused public attention on the new medium.[40] By 1950, television had easily eclipsed radio as the American public's primary source of entertainment and information.

Television copied much from radio during its formative years. Just as radio had been inspired in seeking novel ways for originating programs, so had television. One novel point of origin became available when television cameras were invited to cover the opening day ceremonies as the House convened the Eightieth Congress on January 3, 1947. Many House members praised the brief departure from tradition—even Sam Rayburn (D-Tex.), shortly to become an ardent foe of congressional television.[41] Ironically, television viewers would not see the House assembled as a deliberative body again for more than three decades.

3 · Televising Congressional Hearings: Acclaim and Controversy

Ralph Goldman surveyed the possibilities for television's role in congressional matters and wrote in 1950, "A new synthesis of legislative process and mass media is in the making and seems only to wait upon the appropriate catalyst, for the elements to be combined are many and the inertia to be overcome is great."[1] Those remarks were profound in at least one respect: It indeed would be many years before the nominal union of television and Congress that had occurred in 1947 would result in actual coverage of House and Senate chamber deliberations. However, television was destined to achieve its first notoriety in a different congressional environment, one better suited for the times to the needs of the television industry and the needs of Congress. Thus, television in 1948 would cover its first congressional committee investigative hearing.

CONGRESSIONAL HEARINGS: FUNCTIONAL OVERVIEW

Deriving its power from the U.S. Constitution, Congress has established the investigative hearing for the following reasons: 1) "Fact-finding for possible special and remedial legislation"; 2) "Fulfilling Congress' function as a 'watchdog' over government operations and programs"; 3) "Resolving questions concerning membership or procedure such as conduct of elections or fitness of members of Congress"; and 4) "Informing the public."[2] The history of congressional investigations, dating from 1792, has often been controversial, traveling what has been described as "an erratic trail, marked by some of the brightest and darkest moments in congressional annals."[3]

Persons both inside and outside of Congress have defended the necessity of investigative hearings. For instance, a judge once wrote, "The right to pass laws necessarily implies the right to obtain information upon any matter which may become the subject of a law."[4] And Sen. Scott W. Lucas (D-Ill.) remarked, "The making of investigations and the creation of good laws for free men are the two essential activities of the Congress. Of these two functions, the exercise of the investigating power must come first. Before we can legislate effectively, we must investigate."[5]

Given one of the primary goals of the investigative hearing, that of informing the public, it seems only natural that television would have become a part of the hearing process. Congressmen who, for whatever reasons, had been inhibited from allowing television to cover their chamber proceedings threw those inhibitions to the wind by allowing live coverage of their hearings. There was the unspoken realization, of course, that such coverage would publicize not only the substance of the hearings but also the participation and to some extent the achievement of those conducting them.

TELEVISED CONGRESSIONAL HEARINGS: ORIGINS

The first reported instance of a televised congressional hearing occurred in 1948 when the Senate Armed Services Committee allowed coverage of its March 30 and April 2 hearings on universal military training. Less than four months later, the House Committee on Un-American Activities (HUAC) allowed telecasting of its hearings regarding claims of communist infiltration of the U.S. Government. Better known as the Hiss-Chambers hearings (for Alger Hiss, an accused U.S. State Department spy, and Whittaker Chambers, his accuser), the televised portion of these hearings lasted for twenty-one days, running from late July through early September 1948. Television covered additional HUAC hearings as the committee spent the remainder of September 1948 investigating communist infiltration of the Hollywood movie industry. Between 1948 and 1951 five other committees, including the Joint Committee on Atomic Energy, the House Committee on Armed Services, the Senate Committee on Banking and Currency, the Senate Committee on Foreign Relations and the Senate Select Committee on Small Business, also allowed television coverage of some portion of investigative hearings they were conducting.[6] A sixth Senate committee, the Kefauver Committee, in 1951 conducted televised hearings that were described by *Life* magazine as "the first big television broadcast of an affair of . . . government, the broadcast from which all future use of television in public affairs must date."[7]

TELEVISED HEARINGS: THE SENATE PERSPECTIVE

The Kefauver Committee Hearings

The Special Senate Committee to Investigate Organized Crime in Interstate Commerce, better known as the Kefauver Committee for its chairman Sen. Estes Kefauver, conducted a series of televised investigative hearings during a two-month period from late January to late March 1951. The investigation keyed on gathering information about this country's network of crime syndicates and the relationships between the syndicates and government officials. Although the committee held hearings in fourteen U.S. cities, television covered only those in New Orleans, Detroit, St. Louis, Los Angeles, San Francisco, New York and Washington, D.C.[8] Public response to the telecasts was phenomenal, as exemplified by one publication's description of how "thousands of letters and phone calls from Detroit residents inundated the studios of WWJ-TV and WJBK-TV, thanking the stations for their part in exposing the face of evil."[9]

The Kefauver Committee's most extensive television exposure occurred in New York City, home of the major kingpins of organized crime and, more important, home of the greatest potential television audience. Five of the seven New York television stations aired all or portions of the eleven days of hearings. The American Broadcasting Corporation (ABC) and Dumont television networks relayed hearings coverage to several of their affiliates in the Northeast. Had the coaxial television cable that eventually linked the East and West coasts been complete, the Kefauver Committee's New York hearings would have had a national television audience. Estimates placed the New York area viewing audience at between 1.5 and 4.5 million during the morning hours and ten million during the evening. Daily routines were upset as housewives formed listening clubs and held television parties, public officials and business executives huddled around available television sets, and motion picture theaters cancelled regularly scheduled movies in deference to their loss of customers to the Kefauver Committee telecasts.[10]

The Kefauver Committee's accomplishments were mixed. Few of the committee's proposals for dealing with organized crime were ever enacted into law. The public that had been so aroused and entranced by televised hearing revelations quickly became apathetic, seeming to treat what had been observed as only ephemeral entertainment. In the context of television programming, the Kefauver Committee was awarded an Emmy by the Academy of Television Arts and Sciences in 1952 for its part in "bringing the working of . . . government into the homes of the American people." In terms of individual accomplishments it might be argued that the political strength of Sen. Estes Kefauver to challenge for the Democratic Party's presidential nomination in 1952 was due to notoriety derived from his television hearings.[11]

An accomplishment of a different sort resulting from the Kefauver Committee was the debate it spawned over television's role in the congressional hearing. The debate was fueled by the refusal of two convicted gamblers, Morris Kleinman and Louis Rothkopf, to testify before the committee during the Washington phase of its hearings. Both men based their refusal on the presence of television cameras in the hearing room, claiming that their " 'constitutional rights' would be violated if compelled to testify while being televised."[12] The day following Kleinman's and Rothkopf's refusal the Kefauver Committee cited both for contempt, and on March 30, 1951, the full Senate upheld the contempt citations.[13]

Ordinarily, the Kleinman and Rothkopf cases would have been transferred directly to a U.S. attorney for prosecution,[14] but the transfer was delayed when Sen. Harry Cain (R-Wash.) introduced a motion on April 2 calling for reconsideration of the Senate's citations vote. Reconsideration would automatically force the Senate to debate the whole issue of televising congressional hearings. Rumor had it that Senator Cain's action was influenced to some degree by television network officials urging key senators "not to force a court test of television's rights to broadcast proceedings without approval of participants."[15] Cain's efforts would therefore be directed toward defusing the television issue by emphasizing the Kefauver Committee's failure to conduct its affairs properly.

Debate over reconsideration of the contempt citations was set for August 10, 1951. Shortly into the debate, Senator Cain assailed the Kefauver Committee:

I was watching the television show, as an average American . . . when Kleinman and Rothkopf refused to answer questions. I was disturbed and shocked, as an American, by the manner in which they were treated. I was reminded of what I assume a people's court in any totalitarian country must be. I saw no effort to get at the truth. It seemed to me that the actors were determined that the show must go on. The performance got out of hand. As I sat and studied this picture of a special committee running wild, I made up my mind to stop a repeat performance if I ever had that chance.[16]

Sen. Alexander Wiley (R-Wis.), a member of the Kefauver Committee, defended the committee's conduct, saying that 99 percent of the correspondence he had received agreed that it had "performed a great and constructive function in the 'national emergency.'" He felt that Kleinman and Rothkopf were using the television issue as a "smoke screen" and that they would have refused to testify regardless of television's presence or absence.[17] Sen. Herbert O'Conor (D-Md.), another committee member, defended Senator Kefauver's handling of the hearings as a "model of decorum, . . . judicial temperament, . . . [and] eminent fairness" and added that "in every case in which television has been used, the chairman has announced . . . that any witness who declined or who did not desire to be televised . . . would not be required to submit to it."[18] Kleinman and Rothkopf evidently had made no such request but had instead chosen to make a grandstand play by challenging the Kefauver Committee's control of its hearing procedures.

Several senators stressed the value of televised hearings and a committee's right to conduct them. Television was praised by Senator Wiley for its ability to extend a hearing beyond the confines of a hearing room, and he lauded the medium as "the greatest single educational arm available to the committee for stirring the public conscience."[19] Senator Kefauver thought it presumptuous of a witness to think he or she could dictate the manner by which a congressional committee chooses to conduct its hearings.[20] If the committee allowed television coverage, witnesses would have to abide by that decision.

After concluding a debate in which numerous questions were raised but few resolved, the Senate again voted to uphold the Kleinman and Rothkopf contempt citations.[21]

Commentary in the Wake of Kefauver Hearings

The Kefauver hearings and the subsequent debate over the issues raised by the Kleinman and Rothkopf cases precipitated a flurry of comments from legal scholars[22] and journalists.[23] Most of the commentary was negative, calling attention to the "morbid curiosity and sensationalism"[24] associated with televising the hearings, or, as someone called it, a "prostitution of the true function of a legislative committee."[25] Another critic used less colorful language to decry what he considered the effects on proceedings that are "carried to the very firesides of all America through nationwide television and radio networks":

By laying undue emphasis on publicizing its investigations, as seems currently in vogue, the congressional investigating committee can all too easily lose sight of its legitimate objective of searching for needed information and thus degenerate the whole proceeding into nothing more than a three-ring circus constituting a mere entertainment spectacle for the public, or a propaganda extravaganza for ambitious politicians.[26]

Criticism of congressional investigations, particularly their methods of operation, did not begin with the Kefauver hearings. According to George B. Galloway, numerous levels of criticism accompanied by proposals for reform predated television by several years.[27] Had it not been for the flagrant disregard for witness rights coupled with excessive procedural abuses that occurred during hearings conducted by the House Un-American Activities Committee,[28] criticism of the Kefauver hearings, following as they did in HUAC's wake, might have been less severe. HUAC had caused such alarm that influential American scholars, journalists, jurists, labor leaders, civic leaders and members of the general public insisted that Congress act somehow to throttle the committee's investigative procedures.[29] As a result, Sen. Scott Lucas introduced a measure (S.Con.Res. 2) in 1949 that would have provided a procedural "code of conduct" for congressional investigative committees. Lucas insisted that he was "deeply aware of the fact that any step toward committee reform must not weaken the powers or the wide range of committee inquiries." Alluding to congressional committees as representing the "eyes and ears of Congress," Lucas said that he had "no intention of attempting to put blinders on the eyes of committee members or stoppers in their ears."[30] Hearings were conducted on S.Con.Res. 2 in late July and early August 1949,[31] but the measure was never reported.

It should be noted that television was neither a central nor a peripheral issue in the 1949 hearings. But, since several days of HUAC hearings had been televised, it might be surmised that at least some of the concern over the committee's activities was due in part to what had been observed on television.

Televised Hearings: Areas of Concern

Television was very much at the center of the Kefauver hearings controversy. Broadly stated, greatest concern seemed to focus on the following questions:

Did the televising of the Kefauver hearings manifest a valuable new ingredient of democratic government? Or did it, rather, exploit and aggravate the sensational features which all too frequently disfigure congressional investigations? What about the rights of the witnesses who were haled before the committee and subjected to the heat, glare, and public exposure of newsreels and television in addition to the barrage of questions from the committee members and counsel?[32]

In the matter of manifesting a "valuable new ingredient of democratic government," televised hearings received mixed reviews. One line of argument suggested that television extended proceedings beyond the close proximity of a committee room and made it "practical for the individual citizen to exercise his right to attend public hearings."[33] A corollary of the "extended hearing" argument was the "right to know" argument, suggesting that the public had a right to receive the kind of information made available during a congressional hearing.[34] One defender of televised hearings even suggested that besides information germane to the subject of the hearings, the public also was able to observe elected officials at work, constructing "a personal record for which they must one day stand up and be counted."[35]

Critics of televised hearings claimed that arguments in favor of such concepts as the "extended hearing" failed to recognize that the role of a public hearing was not so much to publicize the event but "to protect the witness from a star chamber proceeding."[36] Also, if there was an assumption that an "extended hearing" via television meant a better-informed public—informed of the subject matter of the hearing, at least—that assumption was not universally shared. Attorney Edward Bennett Williams, for instance, remarked that "ten times more useless, irrelevant, repetitive and inane questions are propounded in the televised hearings than in those not televised. Everybody must get on camera. The important thing is to be seen and heard, not to further the legislative purpose of the inquiry."[37]

As for the "right to know" argument, writer Richard Rovere remarked,

The "right to know" is . . . nothing more than a loose restatement of the idea of a right of inquiry—itself an extension, or interpretation, of freedom of speech, the press, and religion, protected by the First

Amendment. No obligation on the part of public men to *satisfy* inquiring reporters can be inferred from the right of the reporters to *pursue* inquiry.[38]

Although Rovere made no such distinction, would he have held that reporters from the broadcast media had rights of inquiry equal to those of the print media? A federal court decision had confirmed such journalistic equality,[39] but there were those who insisted that the two media were quite different and that the electronic paraphernalia normally accompanying a broadcast news reporter had more likelihood of disturbing the decorum of a congressional hearing than did the print media reporter with his notepad.[40] There were also those critics who, caring little about how hearings were covered, blamed the press in general for ignoring the civil rights of hearing witnesses while being "zealous and uncompromising" in attempting to satisfy the demands of an "American public voracious for news as it is made."[41]

Ignorance of civil rights was a *cause célèbre* for critics of televised congressional hearings, most of whom claimed that committees conducting such hearings failed to provide due process for witnesses. Legal authorities have defined "due process" in various ways, but as applied here it was "interpreted to mean that the Government, including all of its branches, is without right to deprive a person of life, liberty, or property by an act that has no reasonable relation to any proper governmental purpose or which is so far beyond the necessity of the case as to be an arbitrary exercise of the governmental power."[42] Forcing a witness to undergo psychological stress was cited by at least one authority as a *prima facie* example of due process deprivation:

The very technique of televising . . . congressional investigations, with all the electronic gadgets, together with the knowledge that virtually all America is observing his every mannerism to interpret it as a possible sign of guilt is such as literally to terrify the average witness. There simply is no justification for increasing a thousandfold the usual fears generated by the limited audience in the average congressional hearing room by projecting such a scene to literally millions of unseen eyes and ears.[43]

Besides violating due process rights, televised hearings were also said to violate the witness's "right of privacy." There was some dispute about the legal foundation for a privacy right, but one legal scholar suggested that the foundation was a substantial one:

Although there is no express constitutional language to support the existence of such a right, its existence is thought "evident" in the Bill of Rights, or found within the framework of the Bill of Rights, or implied by the entire Constitution, since it is a "fundamental" right having natural law origins similar to those influential throughout the Constitution.[44]

Most violative of civil rights, though, was that a congressional committee could, as Joseph M. Snee contended, force a witness "to submit against his will to televising and broadcasting":

The committee has the lawful power to make [the witness] available for the giving of testimony, even in public and before newsmen. But it does not have the power to restrain him in his liberty of movement for the purpose of televising him or broadcasting his words—an action whose sole purpose is to *publicize* his testimony and to educate the American public.[45]

The Kleinman-Rothkopf Decision

The Kleinman and Rothkopf cases were combined and tried in U.S. District Court, District of Columbia. On October 6, 1952, Judge Henry Schweinhaut ruled that "the refusal of the defendants to testify was justified," since the crowd, commotion and presence of television and newsreel cameras, microphones, etc. might needlessly have distracted them. After all, declared the judge, "The only reason for having a witness on the stand, either before a committee of Congress or before a court, is to get a thoughtful, calm, considered and, it is to be hoped, truthful disclosure of facts."[46]

The *Kleinman* decision was greeted rather ambiguously. It was subsequently cited by some jurists as an important legal precedent[47] and perhaps as a resolution to questions raised about the propriety of televising congressional hearings.[48] But the decision seemed to be based quite narrowly, applying only to the issues of the immediate case. Most important, the decision neither stated nor implied a constitutional basis for prohibiting television coverage of congressional hearings. As noted in one analysis of the decision, "the defendants were upheld in their refusal to testify because of a general lack of decorum in the hearing room. In all probability, the decision would have been the same in the absence of television."[49] Moreover, because "courts have no authority to speak or act upon the conduct by the legislative branch of its own business, so long as the bounds of power and pertinency are not exceeded,"[50] Judge Schweinhaut was wise to have steered clear of directly addressing whether Congress could or even should be using television during its hearing proceedings.

Congressional Hearing: Grand Jury or Trial?

One of the most serious complaints about congressional hearings was the inquisitional posture they oftentimes assumed, giving them the appearance of a grand jury or even a full-scale trial. As Telford Taylor remarked in reference to the Kefauver hearings:

It is fundamental . . . that [no witness] was on trial and that the hearings were in no sense a judicial proceeding. Yet, indubitably, thousands of people who read the newspapers or watched the television screen assumed or concluded that the hearings indeed constituted a trial. Even journalistic comment on the hearings has been replete with references to the trial, court attendants and other verbiage suggestive of judicial proceedings. . . .

These misunderstandings, indeed, are the basis of one of the objections most strongly raised against televising the hearings. It is argued that television gave wide currency to the erroneous notion that the guilt or innocence of [witnesses] was being adjudicated.[51]

Two important distinctions were drawn between grand jury hearings and congressional investigative hearings. First, the function of the grand jury hearing is "to inquire into specific violations of law," while the function of the congressional hearing is "to inquire into general conditions." Second, the grand jury hearing is conducted in secrecy so that unfounded accusations against persons—either witnesses themselves or individuals not present—may be dismissed without publicity.[52] Unfounded accusations arising during a congressional hearing, especially when televised, were noted as particularly odious due to the "immediacy with which television can circulate injury to the reputation and property of those persons drawn even incidentally within the compass of the investigations."[53]

Army-McCarthy Hearings

At least one observer who had been keeping an eye on the activities of Sen. Joseph McCarthy (R-Wis.) predicted that the senator would someday put on a "show" that would make the efforts of the Kefauver Committee "look like the work of inept amateurs."[54] Given the controversy that erupted following the Kefauver hearings, it is difficult to imagine how, in less than three years, the Senate would have consented to what would become the Army-McCarthy hearings.

Senator McCarthy entered the national limelight on February 9, 1950, when he delivered a speech in Wheeling, West Virginia, charging that known members of the Communist Party were being harbored in the U.S. State Department.[55] Three years later, McCarthy was named chairman of the Senate Committee on Government Operations and of its Permanent Subcommittee on Investigations with "broad statutory power to investigate the functioning of every part of the executive branch."[56] Utilizing his chairmanship to its fullest, McCarthy was said to have "cajoled and threatened subpoenaed witnesses, intimidated elected officials," and to have "ultimately questioned the loyalty of the leadership of the U.S. Army."[57]

The Army-McCarthy hearings equalled, if not surpassed, the Kefauver hearings in notoriety. Beginning on April 22, 1954, and ending on June 17, the hearings ran thirty-six days and consumed approximately 187 broadcast hours. The basic matter ostensibly under investigation was the responsibility for what Senator McCarthy perceived as communist infiltration of the U.S. armed forces. The ABC and Dumont networks broadcast the hearings in full; NBC carried the first two days and then opted for filmed highlights thereafter; and CBS carried only filmed highlights from the beginning. ABC-TV fed the hearings to a total of ninety-two stations, thirteen of which were NBC affiliates that picked up the ABC feed after NBC had discontinued live coverage. Some thirty million persons viewed the opening proceedings on April 22, with an estimated three million families watching the hearings at any given moment.[58]

The Army-McCarthy hearings epitomized a style of examination that perhaps reached its perfection at the hands of Senator McCarthy. Commenting on that style, newsman Edward R. Murrow said, "No one familiar with the history of this country can deny that congressional committees are useful. It is necessary to investigate before legislating. But the line between investigation and persecuting is a very fine one, and the junior senator from Wisconsin has stepped over it repeatedly."[59]

Committee Code of Fair Practices

Reaction to the Army-McCarthy hearings was mixed. At least one opinion poll showed the public viewing Senator McCarthy as a courageous defender of Americanism; but the senator's colleagues felt otherwise, voting to censure him only a short time after the hearings ended.[60] Along with condemnation of McCarthy came condemnation of his committee's conduct. There appeared a consensus that Senate committees needed a general code of standards of fair practices to govern the manner in which they conducted investigative hearings.

The suggestion that such a code be adopted either by statute or standing rules was nothing new. Since the 1930s, bills had been introduced in both the House and Senate calling for either a mandatory or voluntary code.[61] Congress gave its first serious consideration in 1949 to a measure (S.Con.Res. 2) introduced by Sen. Scott Lucas that would have created a "code of fair play." Testifying in behalf of his resolution, Senator Lucas made a profound prediction that there would be "no relief . . . from the intrigues of government in the days to come and, therefore, there will probably be more and more investigations as time goes on, and the more investigations you have, the more reason there will be for the passage of a resolution such as I have submitted."[62] The Lucas resolution failed, but it did generate considerable discussion and support both in the press and in legal circles.[63]

The Kefauver Committee hearings reignited concern that a code be established. And once again hearings were conducted on the subject, this time by the Senate Committee on Expenditures in the Executive Departments in June 1951. Conspicuous by its absence during hearings on the Lucas bill was any attention to the televising of hearings. This was not the case in 1951. Though television was only one item among many proposed to be covered in a code of standards,[64] it did receive major attention. The testimony of Sen. Estes Kefauver was especially noteworthy. He remarked that he himself would soon introduce a bill that would establish a broad general code, a portion of which would deal with committee use of television, leaving specific code application to individual committee chairmen.[65]

A brief word of explanation about committee procedures must be included here. The U.S. Constitution, Article I, Section 5, Clause 2, asserts that "each house [of Congress] may determine the rules of its proceedings." Implicit in this language is the freedom—but not the requirement—for adopting either formal or informal rules of committee procedure. Committees by the late 1940s were adopting a variety of rules,[66] some of which were supplemented with informal policy decisions that either opened or closed committee proceedings to television. The Kefauver Committee itself had adopted a policy designed "to avoid unfair discrimination between the various news media and at the same time to avoid subjecting the witness to an ordeal that would unduly interfere with the giving of his testimony."[67] Although the committee generally ignored the impact television might have had on witnesses during most of its hearings, committee members eventually became more cognizant of that impact. In an interim report released in May 1951, the Kefauver Committee stated its feelings that "a code of congressional procedure should be worked out so as . . . to insure the continuing dignity and maximum effectiveness of legislative proceedings which might be televised as well as to preserve the constitutional rights of citizens."[68] The committee reiterated those feelings in its final report and included a lengthy analysis of the important role television had played in the committee's hearings.[69]

By mid-1952, nearly twenty bills had been introduced in Congress calling for reform of congressional investigation procedures and creation of a procedural code of fair practices. Many of the proposed codes were modeled after the one adopted by the Investigations Subcommittee of the Senate Committee on Expenditures in the Executive Department. One of the provisions of that code read, "If the witness so requests, no photographs, moving pictures, television or radio broadcasts of the proceeding shall be permitted while the witness is testifying."[70]

Congressional committee codes of fair practices were subjects for concern outside Congress as well. The New York State Bar Association, in 1952, recommended that Congress adopt such a code,[71] and in 1953 the American Civil Liberties Union adopted a "Statement of Principle and Desirable Practice," part of which read, "The ACLU, after consideration of the desirability of both freedom of communication and the safeguarding of due process, believes that proper rules for the conduct of legislative hearings should be adopted and a satisfactory practice established before the filming, broadcasting and televising of such hearings is permitted." The ACLU also urged that television networks adopt reportorial and editorial rules of their own for covering congressional hearings. Recommended provisions in these rules would allow telecasting of responses by persons attacked or mentioned unfavorably by witnesses during hearings; would require identification of any hearing as a legislative and not a judicial proceeding; and would require fair treatment by directors in terms of camera shots.[72]

Attention to adopting a code of fair practices intensified following the Army-McCarthy hearings. Public concern that Congress use "fair and just investigating methods" was an especially strong motivation for legislative action.[73] Eight Senate bills on the matter (S.Res. 65, 146, 223, 249, 253, 256 and S.Con.Res. 11 and 86) were introduced during the Eighty-third Congress.[74] Beginning in late June and continuing periodically through August 1954, the Senate Rules and Administration Committee conducted hearings on the bills.[75]

The committee's subsequent report noted in part several suggestions for using television to cover hearings. One was to "forbid coverage completely," another was to "permit coverage under appropriate technical safeguards," a third was to "permit unlimited access," and a fourth was to "forbid coverage by television and motion-picture cameras during the testimony of a witness who objects." Several Senate committees had already adopted informal rules incorporating the fourth alternative. The report concluded with the following recommendation: "That the Senate adopt the rule that a witness may request, on grounds of distraction, harassment, or physical discomfort, that during his testimony, television, motion picture, and other cameras and lights not be directed at him, such request to be ruled on by the committee members present at the hearing."[76]

A resolution (S.Res. 17) incorporating the Rules Committee's recommendation accompanied the committee's report. However, there was no action on the matter during the remainder of the Eighty-fourth Congress. What's more, no serious attempt would ever again be made to fashion a Senate committee code of fair practices. Henceforth, rules pertaining to use of television would be those either formally or informally adopted by each Senate committee.

TELEVISED HEARINGS: THE HOUSE PERSPECTIVE

Efforts toward adopting a committee code of fair practices also were under way in the U.S. House, particularly during the Eighty-third and Eighty-fourth Congresses.[77] Not only were these efforts unsuccessful, they were unnecessary given the status of televised House hearings.

While the Senate was realizing the publicity value in televising its committee hearings, Speaker of the House Sam Rayburn ruled in February 1952 that television cameras henceforth would be banned from House committee hearings. The ban originated with the Speaker's rescinding a House Select Committee's plans to televise its hearings on the Katyn Forest Massacre. Several days later, Speaker Rayburn also rescinded plans for the House Un-American Activities Committee—a committee that heretofore had coveted the publicity value of televised hearings—to televise a series of hearings in Detroit, Michigan. This action prompted a parliamentary inquiry from Rep. Joseph Martin (R-Mass.) as to what authority the Speaker had to cancel hearing telecasts. To this, Speaker Rayburn replied:

The Chair is operating under the rules of the House. One of the rules reads as follows: "The rules of the House are hereby made the rules of its standing committees so far as applicable."
There is no authority, and as far as the Chair knows, there is no rule granting the privilege of television of the House of Representatives, and the Chair interprets that as applying to these committees or subcommittees, whether they sit in Washington or elsewhere.

When Representative Martin suggested that the House adopt a rule allowing televised coverage of its committee hearings, Speaker Rayburn agreed that a rule-making was in order and that if one were adopted he would enforce it.[78] Subsequently, on February 27, 1952, Rep. George Meader (R-Mich.) introduced a resolution (H.Res. 540) to create a rule "which would clearly vest in committees of the House the authority to permit telecasting of proceedings, in the discretion of such committees."[79] The likelihood that his resolution would pass was understood by Meader to be remote at best. The House Rules Committee, to which the bill was submitted, was known for its reluctance to change procedural rules.[80] Furthermore, overcoming the power of the Speaker, whose influence in these matters was traditional and who obviously opposed television anyway, would be a formidable task. Sure enough, the Rules Committee never considered H.Res. 540.

The Rayburn ban was criticized not only by the Speaker's House colleagues but also by persons outside the House. The Detroit Common (or City) Council passed a resolution requesting that the ban be lifted, especially for the scheduled Detroit HUAC hearings.[81] The Executive Committee of the Radio Correspondents' Galleries of the U.S. Capitol wrote a letter to Speaker Rayburn objecting to his decision as depriving radio and television reporters of the use of the tools of their trade to cover congressional hearings.[82] The Speaker remained unmoved.

Why Speaker Rayburn so strongly opposed televising House hearings is uncertain. One source cited several possible reasons, one being Rayburn's distrust for the media in general and for television in particular. A second was his disdain for the way television had been used in the Senate to elevate individuals like Estes Kefauver into congressional leadership roles and even into contention for the presidency. A third reason, closely tied to the second, was the opportunity television afforded young House members to be seen and heard in a manner the cherished congressional seniority system had never allowed.[83]

Whatever the reasons for his ban, Speaker Rayburn could not continue its enforcement when he briefly lost the Speakership to Joseph Martin during the Eighty-third Congress. Speaker Martin lifted the ban from 1953 through 1954, but when Rayburn regained the Speaker's chair in 1955, the ban was reinstated.[84]

The decision was protested immediately. First, requests were sent from the National Association of Radio Television Broadcasters and the Radio-Television Correspondents' Association asking that the Speaker reconsider.[85] Next, Rep. George Meader introduced H.Res. 99, an identical bill to his unsuccessful H.Res. 540 introduced three years earlier. Calling attention to a recently televised presidential press conference, Meader made what would become a familiar appeal for passage of his measure: "If House committees are denied the very powerful media of communication of live or recorded broadcasting and telecasting, . . . the public will come to know less and less of the activities of the House and its committees as compared with the activities of the Senate and its committees and the activities of the executive branch of the Government."[86]

Representative Meader continued his efforts a few days later by making another parliamentary inquiry of the Speaker regarding his committee television ruling. Speaker Rayburn responded by referring to his previous pronouncement on the subject. Essentially, said the Speaker, "the Chair still thinks that it is not in accordance with the rules of the House of Representatives or its committees to televise or broadcast hearings or actions before any committee of the House, and so holds and will hold unless and until the rules of the House are amended."[87] At the conclusion of the Speaker's remarks, "thunderous applause from the majority side of the House" is said to have erupted.[88]

By early March 1955, the House Rules Committee had scheduled hearings on Representative Meader's H.Res. 99. Since emotion rather than logic appeared to dominate committee testimony, proponents of rules to allow televised House hearings were unconvincing. One week after hearings had begun, the committee decided not to recommend any changes in House rules.[89]

The only serious challenge to confront the Rayburn House television ban in terms of flagrant defiance of the Speaker's ruling occurred in June 1957. Representative Francis Walter (D-Pa.), a HUAC subcommittee chairman, allowed live local telecasts of subcommittee hearings being conducted in San Francisco. A "transcontinental sparring match" erupted between Speaker Rayburn and Chairman Walter as to the interpretation of Rayburn's 1955 ruling. Walter claimed the ruling had been made during the previous Congress and was not effective during the Eighty-fifth Congress.[90] The Speaker, incensed by Walter's insubordination, invoked his power to throttle the challenge by declaring, "There will not be any more (House) Committee or Subcommittee hearings in Washington, or anywhere else televised or broadcast by radio. Period!"[91]

During the first half of the next decade, the House Rules Committee conducted two more series of hearings on the House television matter. The first came in February 1961, as Representative Meader's H.Res. 173 was considered.[92] The second came in March 1963, as H.Res. 263, introduced by Rep. Oren Harris (D-Ark.) was being considered.[93] Both resolutions dealt with providing televised coverage of House committee proceedings. The committee voted not to report the Meader Resolution, although the eight-to-six count was surprisingly close.[94] The Rules Committee similarly failed to report the Harris Resolution.

Any hope that televised House hearings might have been implemented in the near future was dashed by the Rules Committee's failure to act on the issue. During the year preceding the committee's inaction, television advocates had harbored some hope that the new Speaker of the House, John McCormack (D-Mass.), would reverse his predecessor's ban, since one of the new

Speaker's first actions was interpreted as a sign of his favorable attitude toward House television. McCormack had agreed to allow live televised coverage of opening ceremonies when the House convened the Eighty-seventh Congress. However, a proviso limited coverage to the Speaker's opening remarks; once House business had begun, the telecast was to cease.[95] On the question of televised House hearings, though, McCormack had remained noncommittal. Some weeks prior to his assuming the Speakership, he had indicated a leaning toward continuation of the Rayburn ban, but he had declined to comment further on the subject until a formal parliamentary inquiry on a new ruling could be made from the House floor.[96]

Representative Meader wasted little time in providing the Speaker an opportunity for that ruling. On January 15, 1962, Meader presented a lengthy brief on the House floor containing items supporting his contention that television cameras should be allowed to cover committee hearings.[97] The next day, Meader made the following formal parliamentary inquiry of Speaker McCormack: "May committees of the House of Representatives, in their discretion, permit telecasting, broadcasting, and photography of their public hearings?" To this the Speaker replied:

The present occupant of the Chair thinks that he should follow precedent and give due consideration to opinions of former Speakers. The Chair thinks that Mr. Speaker Rayburn's opinions were well considered and the Chair intends to follow those opinions until such time as the House, by its own action in amending its rules, provides for a different method of proceeding.[98]

Several members of the House greeted Speaker McCormack's ruling with the same applause that had greeted Speaker Rayburn's original pronouncement in 1955.[99]

For eight more years the House ban would remain in effect. But, eventually, television would have its way. Passage of the Legislative Reorganization Act of 1970 (to be discussed at length in the next chapter) not only opened the way for televised House hearings but also established a limited procedural code to regulate the telecasts.

TELEVISING CONGRESSIONAL CHAMBER PROCEEDINGS

The attention that focused on telecasts of congressional committee proceedings following the Army-McCarthy hearings naturally spilled over occasionally to include telecasts of congressional chamber deliberations. After all, "many of the basic policy considerations [applied] to both; namely, secrecy vs. publicity; individual rights vs. public interest and participation; and, particularly, efficiency vs. public participation."[100] There was, nonetheless, little congressional incentive to regard television as a legitimate tool of the legislative process. Robert E. Summers surveyed the languid state of congressional (or "legislative," as he called it) broadcasting in 1955 and unbeknownst to him characterized it in a manner that would remain constant for many years to come. Said Summers,

The tide of opinion is running strongly against legislative broadcasting in Congress and there is little hope for a change in attitude in the forseeable future. This automatically raises the question as to the desirability of a change, whether, under the circumstances, legislative broadcasting has any practical merit. The answer lies in the optimistic sentiments of the little handful of television's adherents in Congress. "The very fact that no previous session of the American Congress has been so closely followed by so many of the nation's citizens is itself a commentary on this miracle of modern communication," said Senator [Andrew] Schoeppel in 1954. The significance of television goes far beyond the spectacular coverage of committee hearings, he added, noting that the important fact was that television "has shown itself to be a valuable new tool of the democratic process itself."[101]

4 · Television Covers House Committees and Watergate Investigations

Events occurring during a period stretching for nearly a decade from the mid–1960s to the mid–1970s had an extraordinary impact on congressional television. The period began with efforts under way by a joint congressional committee to allow statutory access of television cameras to House committee proceedings; it concluded with television assuming a prominent role in providing America a close-up view of the Watergate hearings and subsequent presidential impeachment debates.

JOINT COMMITTEE ON THE ORGANIZATION OF CONGRESS

Early in the first session of the Eighty-ninth Congress both the Senate and the House turned toward establishing a Joint Committee on the Organization of Congress. The committee was authorized to make a thorough study of all phases of congressional operation and wherever necessary to recommend improvements in those operations.[1] It would function as a successor to the LaFollette-Monroney Committee of the 1940s. In fact, Sen. Mike Monroney, now the senior senator from Oklahoma, had originated the idea for the new committee. A comprehensive review of all congressional procedures, according to the senator, would be fashioned around specific attention to overhauling the antiquated congressional appropriations process.[2]

Six members of each congressional house comprised the twelve-member joint committee. Senator Monroney was selected to co-chair from the Senate side; Rep. Ray Madden (D-Ind.) was chosen from the House side. The committee would be prohibited from making recommendations on specific rule changes affecting either house; rather, reports of committee findings and general recommendations would be referred to the rules committees of the two houses for appropriate action.[3]

The committee began public hearings on May 10, 1965, and eventually heard nearly two hundred witnesses.[4] Though not a major agenda item, congressional television nonetheless received its most critical appraisal since mid–1955. That the committee appeared so solicitous toward the subject might be attributed to the presence of former Rep. George Meader as a committee counsel. Meader had been an ardent supporter of congressional television while a member of the House.

No less than a dozen congressmen and organization representatives testified in favor of some form of congressional television implementation.[5] Among the several suggestions were those of Sen. Ralph Yarborough (D-Tex.)[6] and Rep. Ed Edmondson (D-Okla.), who proposed a closed-circuit television system by which congressmen could monitor floor activity in either the Senate or House.[7] Sen. Jacob Javits (D-N.Y.) proposed that "great debates" be televised from the congressional floor. Such debates would occur periodically and cover issues of current importance.[8] Rep. Weston Vivian (D-Mich.) proposed recording congressional sessions in order to have a more accurate account of floor proceedings than provided by the *Congressional Record*.[9]

Written testimony presented to the committee explored additional dimensions of the issue. In particular was a survey recently conducted among eighty House members to ascertain attitudes toward certain congressional reform items. One item would have allowed televised House committee hearings by majority consent of committee members. Fifty-five percent of the respondents supported the idea; 43 percent opposed it. Regardless of the apparent support, only 15 percent felt that a measure proposing television coverage of committee hearings had any chance of House passage within the next decade.[10]

After more than a year, the joint committee reported numerous recommendations for reorganizing Congress. Among them were the following:

> 1. Hearings shall be open to the public except when a majority of the committee determines that testimony may either bear on national security matters or tend to reflect adversely on the character or reputation of the witness or others.
> 2. Hearings may be televised and broadcast at the option of the chairman with the approval of a majority of the committee under such rules as the committee may impose to insure fair treatment to all concerned.

Elaborating on its recommendations, the committee said,

We do not favor a rigid rule that either prohibits or requires televised hearings. Each case should be decided on its own merits. The chairman of the committee, with the concurrence of a majority of its members, should be empowered to determine whether television coverage of the hearings is to be allowed. It may not always be appropriate. The committee should insist on fair coverage of all sides of an issue. Modern techniques permit such coverage without destroying the dignity of the proceedings and the committee should insist that those techniques be utilized.[11]

The joint committee noted that if implementation of its recommendations were to occur, it should be gradual and that some structure should be created to oversee the process. The committee further noted that several witnesses had "urged that provision be made for continuing examination of the organization and operations of the Congress, with a view to recommending changes that would help keep the Congress in step with modern and rapidly changing techniques."[12] To that end, the committee recommended creation of a Joint Committee on Congressional Operations with virtually the same objectives as those given the Joint Committee on the Organization of Congress. Some of the suggested areas of study for the proposed committee would be "public televising of [congressional] floor proceedings [and] closed circuit TV or other communications between the floor and Members' offices and committee rooms."[13]

Most of the recommendations contained in the 1966 joint committee report were incorporated into a bill (S.355) and introduced in the Senate in early 1967. The bill won approval after seventeen days of debate, but certain provisions made its passage in the House more difficult. The House Rules Committee failed to act on the measure before the Ninetieth Congress adjourned.[14]

Legislative Reorganization Act and House Television

Congressional reform remained on the agenda as the Ninety-first Congress convened in 1969. In April, the Special Subcommittee on Legislative Reorganization was set up by the House Rules Committee to study provisions of the now dead S.355 for incorporation into a "clean" House bill. Drafting the bill would be the responsibility of the subcommittee, chaired by Rep. B. F. Sisk (D-Calif.) and composed of Representatives Richard Bolling (D-Mo.), John Young (D-Tex.), H. Allen Smith (R-Calif.) and Delbert Latta (R-Ohio).[15]

The subcommittee conducted extensive hearings on several media-related issues on November 6, 1969. Most witnesses were associated with the broadcasting industry in some capacity. Included were National Association of Broadcasters (NAB) President Vincent Wasilewski; John Lynch from ABC News, Bill Small from CBS News and Frank Jordan from NBC News—all directors of their respective networks' Washington news bureaus; Bill Roberts, Radio-Television News Directors Association President; and CBS news reporter Roger Mudd.

As would be expected from this gathering, testimony favored full broadcast access to all congressional proceedings. Views of some of the subcommittee members, however, ran counter to those of the witnesses. Representative Latta in particular chided the broadcast industry in reply to Mr. Wasilewski's opening statement that a "fully informed public is the fundamental strength of our form of government." Latta maintained that only the glamorous committees, sensational issues, and controversial congressmen would attract television cameras. Wasilewski partially agreed but managed to sidestep the issue by saying, "I think this has always been a problem of news reporting, whatever the media would be. I do believe that the public would get more information if the House proceedings were as open as are some of the Senate committee hearings."[16]

Representative Latta raised the selective coverage issue a second time while questioning Mr. Mudd. This time, Latta complained of the networks' practice of concentrating on the chairman of a committee and of representing the chairman's views as those of his entire committee. To this, Mr. Mudd responded:

You try consciously to act for all points of view. It does happen . . . that some or all the differing points of view are held by men of unequal stature. What you look for is the significant point of view from the man who has some influence in the House. You are limited as to how much of a hearing you can put on and you are looking for the man on the committee you know to be powerful and know to sway votes.[17]

John Lynch testified that the subcommittee's draft bill requirement that live broadcasts of committee hearings be uninterrupted was impractical. The good judgment of broadcast journalists, said Lynch, "requires us to report the important, to digest the less important, and to explain to the audience those intricate matters that come before [committees]." He predicted that broadcasters would cover few House hearings unless the restrictive provision were removed.

Lynch opposed another draft bill provision stating that "radio and television tapes [of committee coverage] may be used only to provide accurate, impartial, and legitimate news and shall not be used to produce an inaccurate or distorted report." He expressed his and his colleagues' resentment for the provision's inference:

It is never our intent to be inaccurate, it is against our policies to distort. At the same time, it is impossible to agree on what is accuracy or what is distortion. Honest men disagree, and do so frequently. Errors of omission or commission to one may be honest reporting to another. . . .

To attempt to have each House committee set its own standards of what constitutes an impartial account is to attempt the impossible and to encourage conditions bordering on censorship.[18]

After hearings had ended, the Special Subcommittee on Legislative Reorganization incorporated its recommendations into a bill (H.R. 17654) that subsequently was reported to the House floor by the parent Rules Committee on June 17, 1970. The report left the subcommittee's televised hearings recommendations intact. In doing so, it cautioned that congressional committees should see that procedural rules safeguarding proper decorum were followed. The report also warned that the Rules Committee would reconsider the entire matter of televised hearings if improper use of hearing films or recordings ever came to its attention.[19]

Debate on H.R. 17654 began in mid-July. Section 116, the portion of H.R. 17654 pertaining to committee broadcasts, was debated on July 20. Stated briefly, Sec. 116 proposed that whenever a House committee hearing is opened to the public, "that hearing may be broadcast by radio or television, or both, under such rules as the committee may adopt." Accompanying provisions prohibited using recordings of hearing sessions as "partisan political campaign material" and required that media personnel covering hearings conduct themselves "in strict conformity with and observance of the acceptable standards of dignity, propriety, courtesy, and decorum traditionally observed by the House." Committee hearings were to be opened to broadcast coverage in whole or in part only upon consent of a majority vote of the committee members. If a committee elected to allow coverage, Sec. 116 required that the committee adopt written rules of procedure for broadcast personnel. These rules could specify whatever the committee desired, but Sec. 116 required that certain provisions be included that would, among other things, prohibit commercial sponsorship of live committee coverage, prohibit coverage of committee witnesses upon their request, restrict the number and placement of television cameras in the hearing room, prohibit the movement of broadcast equipment while a hearing is in progress, and limit to the bare minimum the amount of additional lighting usually required to properly illuminate hearing rooms for television coverage. This portion of H.R. 17654, once approved, not only would end the ban on televising House hearings that had originated with Speaker Sam Rayburn but would establish the code of fair procedures (albeit a minimal one) for those telecasts—something the Senate had failed to do during the 1950s.

Debate on Sec. 116 was fairly brief, although support for an amendment introduced by Rep. David Dennis (R-Ind.) showed that strong opposition to televised hearings remained. Dennis's amendment would have deleted Sec. 116 in its entirety. He defended his so-called public interest amendment as necessary if the House hoped ever again to transact "the public business . . . in an efficient manner." Both the House and the public would be better off, argued Dennis, without television cameras in hearing rooms. The amendment failed but by a slim 93-to-96 margin.[20]

With debate concluded, the House voted 326 to 19 on September 17 to send H.R. 17654 to the Senate.[21] After a brief floor debate and some minor amendments the Senate passed H.R. 17654 by a vote of 59 to 5.[22] On October 8, the House accepted the Senate amendments and sent the bill to the President for his signature.[23] And on October 26, H.R. 17654 became Public Law (P.L.) 91-510, the Legislative Reorganization Act of 1970.[24]

Besides the committee television provisions, provisions also existed in the new law for establishing a Joint Committee on Congressional Operations. The committee's duties would be precisely those suggested originally by the Joint Committee on the Organization of Congress in 1966.[25] Within four years, the Joint Committee on Congressional Operations would commence hearings that would lead to yet another milestone for congressional television.

House committees wasted little time in opening their hearings to television. During 1971, the year P.L. 91-510 became effective, hearings were televised or recorded on more than thirty occasions. Some committee members continued to grumble, but television generally was well received.[26]

CONGRESSIONAL ACCESS TO TELEVISION

The 1970 Legislative Reorganization Act now allowed House and Senate committees the freedom to invite television news reporters and camera crews to cover their hearings, but it could not demand that coverage. Outside the hearing room, congressmen were excluded even more from television access privileges. For some time sentiment for guaranteed access had been growing among a small faction in Congress, but efforts toward mandating that guarantee did not surface officially until numerous presidential television appeals for support of this country's Vietnam War effort forced the issue.

Congress, the President and the Fairness Doctrine

The Vietnam War was a divisive issue in this country throughout much of the 1960s. Opposition to it had forced President Johnson from seeking reelection in 1968 and had built support for candidate Richard Nixon, who claimed to have had a "secret plan" to end it. One year after President Nixon's inauguration, however, the conflict had increased its intensity. During that period, from November 1969 through July 1970, the President preempted prime-time network television programming eleven times for press conferences or formal addresses devoted primarily to explaining and seeking support for his war policies.[27]

A number of anti-war groups protested the President's policies but could not gain comparable network television exposure to air their views. Among the protestors was a group of fourteen U.S. Senators who had sponsored a Senate Amendment to End the War to be attached to the Military Procurement Authorization Act (H.R. 17123).[28] Known as the McGovern-Hatfield Amendment for its authors, Senators George McGovern (D-S.Dak) and Mark Hatfield (R-Ore.), the measure was introduced only one day before a presidential prime-time, three-network television appearance to announce that American troops had entered Cambodia. The next day, Senator McGovern requested network time to urge support for his and Senator Hatfield's amendment. Both CBS and ABC refused to supply any time, but NBC agreed to sell the Senator a half hour. McGovern and his thirteen Senate colleagues purchased the time and made their appeal. Soon afterwards, the President made another prime-time, three-network appearance in which he criticized the fourteen senators and, more specifically, the McGovern-Hatfield Amendment. Senator McGovern again requested television time to reply but was rejected by all three networks. The networks based their decisions on what they considered adequate coverage already given the war issue in numerous news and public affairs programs.[29]

The senators subsequently filed a complaint with the Federal Communications Commission alleging violation of the Fairness Doctrine by the three major television networks and their owned and operated stations. Declaring that the President's speeches had presented only one side of a controversial issue, the senators requested that the FCC "require networks to provide time to any substantial group of Senators opposing the President's views on a controversial issue of national importance whenever the issue is one in which the Senate has a role to perform in seeking resolution of the issue, and the President has initiated debate via national television."[30]

The FCC responded on August 14, 1970, by rejecting the senators' request and holding that the networks had acted "reasonably" in denying them time. The FCC agreed that presidential addresses on controversial issues of public importance did trigger a right to reply under the Fairness Doctrine, but broadcast licensees had the discretionary privilege of choosing the proper spokesman to present opposing views. The Commission found no merit in singling out the fourteen senators as a privileged class to whom reply time must be granted.[31] Moreover, the FCC said that issues rather than personalities were at the root of the Fairness Doctrine. A balanced presentation of all sides of an issue was cited as of particular importance. In this respect, the Commission felt that the networks' numerous news items, interview programs and documentaries on the Vietnam War presented a balance to President Nixon's remarks on the subject.[32]

Statutory Congressional Television Access Time

While the quest for an FCC Fairness Doctrine ruling was in progress, Sen. William Fulbright (D-Ark.) selected an alternate method for attempting to secure congressional television access time. His approach was to legislate what he termed "public service time" by amending the 1934 Communications Act. To accomplish this, Fulbright introduced S.J.Res. 209 in June 1970. The resolution read, in part:

[Broadcast] licensees shall provide a reasonable amount of public service time to authorized representatives . . ., to present the views of the Senate and the House of Representatives on issues of public importance. The public service time required to be provided . . . shall be made available to each such authorized representative at least, but not limited to, four times during each calendar year.

The Fulbright measure symbolized frustration among certain members of Congress who saw no alternative but to legislate that congressional views be televised. Several years earlier, Senator Fulbright had seen firsthand the selectivity of networks in covering matters related to the Vietnam War. The occasion was the February 1966 Senate Foreign Relations Committee's Vietnam hearings, hearings that were described by David Halberstam as a "landmark event"—"a constitutional confrontation of the first order" that "ended more than a generation of assumed executive branch omniscience in foreign policy, and congressional acquiescence to that omniscience."[33] As important as these hearings were, none of the television networks carried them in full. There was certainly valid justification for not airing every minute of the several days of testimony, but it was charged by then CBS News President Fred Friendly that his network had made an economic rather than public interest decision in refraining from covering more of the hearings than Friendly felt it should. CBS had decided instead to air reruns of "I Love Lucy," "The Real McCoys" and "Andy of Mayberry." That decision was seen by Friendly as so flagrant a violation of network responsibility and principle that he resigned in protest.[34]

Senate Joint Resolution 209 was referred to the Senate Commerce Committee's Communications Subcommittee, where hearings on the measure were scheduled for August 4, 5 and 6—little more than a week before the FCC issued its decision on the McGovern request for access time. Senator Fulbright opened the hearings by comparing the fragmented comments allowed congressmen during television news and interview programs with the kind of attention given the President. The President, said Fulbright, had "something close to the functional equivalent of exclusive access" to prime-time television. The Senator then underscored the constitutional equality of the two governmental branches—an equality that he felt should apply as well to their ability to communicate:

> Under our Constitution there is no paramount branch of the Federal Government; if indeed the framers regarded any branch as primus inter pares, it was not the Executive but the Congress, whose powers are spelled out in the Constitution at greatest length and in the greatest detail. If the President is regarded as having the right to communicate with the people through the mass media whenever he wishes, the spirit and intent of our Constitution require that no less a privilege be accorded to the Senate and the House of Representatives—or, if it should claim it, to the judiciary.[35]

Senate Joint Resolution 209 would go far beyond mere privilege, though. According to Fulbright, the resolution's intent was to mandate a *"Congressional right of access to the mass media."* (Emphasis added.) Moreover, suggested the senator, "Broadcast time should be available to the Congress at all times and not simply in order to reply when the President speaks to the nation. The purpose is not to facilitate the expression of partisan views on national issues but to guarantee the right of the people to hear diverse and opposing views regardless of party."[36]

Senator Fulbright's "right of access" concept was attacked immediately by representatives of the broadcast media. Frank Stanton of CBS said it would "violate the intent and spirit of the first amendment." And, he added,

> Surely a legislative requirement which would afford to officials of the executive branch of the Government, and only to such officials, compelled access to the broadcast media, would be widely regarded as discriminatory and improper. It seems to me that a legislative enactment which would provide such mandatory access to radio and television only for members of the legislative branch of the Government is hardly less objectionable. Such an enactment would presume—for the first time in American history—that incumbent members of the Federal legislature have a privileged status over all other American citizens, in or out of office, in utilizing organs of information. This idea, I believe, would be highly repugnant to the American people.[37]

Theodore Pierson, Counsel for the Republican National Committee, shared Stanton's feelings toward what he termed the "new and radical doctrine of right-of-access." "One of the unique characteristics of our system of broadcast regulation," said Pierson, "is that the Government except under its war powers, has no right to command [broadcast] licensees to carry Government programs."[38]

Besides the philosophical questions raised by S.J.Res. 209, there was the practical matter of selecting someone to represent congressional views. Senator Fulbright suggested that the congressional majority and minority leaders could choose spokesmen, choices that would be simplified by the natural emergence of advocates for various points of view.[39] But Leonard Goldenson, President of ABC, disagreed: "Experience indicates that the greater the controversy surrounding an issue, the more fragmented and divergent are the views of those who comprise the Senate and House."[40]

There were other problems. How, for instance, would the Fairness Doctrine and the equal opportunities provisions of the Communications Act apply to congressional appearances sanctioned under S.J.Res. 209? NAB President Vincent Wasilewski remarked that unless "exclusionary legislation" were adopted by Congress, broadcasters would be required to balance congressional appearances with appearances by spokesmen presenting opposing views whenever controversial matters were addressed. Moreover, appearances by congressmen who were announced candidates for reelection would require broadcasters to offer equal time to the congressmen's opponents.[41]

The extensive coverage given the S.J.Res. 209 hearings in the trade press reflected the matter's importance to broadcasters.[42] The pro-industry *Broadcasting* magazine capped its appraisal of the measure with a stinging editorial, charging that "attempts by politicians to capture the medium of television for their private use [had] reached the stage of unembarrassed flagrancy."[43]

Senate Joint Resolution 209 never moved beyond the Communications subcommittee. Its demise was due in large part to the impracticality of selecting spokesmen to represent the views of the entire congressional membership. But the delicate constitutional balance that would have been upset by replacing journalistic discretion with statutory requirements doubtless did little to enhance the measure's chances of passage. Added to these was the partisan complexion of the resolution. Though Fulbright argued to the contrary—"As strongly as possible," he said, "it should be emphasized that the focus of this bill is institutional and not partisan"[44]—the fact remained that anti-war proponents such as himself as well as a Democratic-controlled Congress would be the immediate beneficiaries of his resolution's enactment. Last but certainly not least were the Fairness Doctrine complications inherent in the provisions of S.J.Res. 209. The Communications Subcommittee hardly could have missed the strong message sent its way by the FCC's decision on the McGovern group complaint, coming as it did shortly after the Subcommittee concluded its hearings. To promote consideration of the Fulbright resolution any further would have meant opening a Fairness Doctrine Pandora's Box that the Communications Subcommittee obviously felt would be best left closed.

TELEVISED SENATE WATERGATE HEARINGS

It is safe to say . . . there never was an investigation like that which delved into the "Watergate affair. . . ." That the two-year period covered by the Watergate investigation was one in which the Executive branch of the government of the United States was all but paralyzed in domestic affairs is irrefutable. And, that the investigation culminated in the resignation of the President certainly was a phenomenon unique in American constitutional history.[45]

That statement by Philip B. Kurland places the Watergate affair into perhaps its most comprehensive perspective. Numerous books and articles have examined the subject of Watergate; some of them have dealt with the personalities involved in the scandal and some have dealt with its historical implications, but none yet has answered the riddle of why the interrelated series of events now collectively referred to as "Watergate" occurred in the first place.

Kurland described Watergate as "a great American tragedy" that "began as a farce that might have been written by George S. Kaufman and played by the Marx brothers." The beginning occurred on June 17, 1972, when five burglars armed with cameras and bugging devices were arrested in the Watergate building's Democratic National Committee offices.[46] The burglars' equipment eventually was traced to the President's reelection committee. From that point, a series of revelations in courtrooms and newspaper reports pointed to illegal activities surrounding President Nixon's 1972 reelection campaign, all apparently orchestrated by the highest authorities in the White House. Before Watergate had subsided, the President had been forced to resign—only one step ahead of impeachment—and many of his assistants had been convicted and sentenced to prison terms.

The Senate Democratic caucus initiated formation of the committee to investigate Watergate early in the Ninety-third Congress. On January 11, 1973, Senate Majority Leader Mike Mansfield (D-Mont.) announced that Sam Ervin (D-N.C.), one of the Senate's leading constitutional authorities, would head the committee.[47] The full Senate gave formal approval on February 7, voting 77 to 0 in favor of S.Res. 60 to empanel the Senate Select Committee on Presidential Campaign Activities.[48] Better known by its more informal title, the Ervin Committee consisted of six other members besides Chairman Ervin. The six who shortly were to become national celebrities included Howard Baker (R-Tenn.), Edward Gurney (R-Fla.), Lowell Weicker (R-Conn.), Herman Talmadge (D-Ga.), Joseph Montoya (D-N.Mex.), and Daniel Inouye (D-Hawaii).[49]

The Ervin Committee began its public hearings on May 17, 1973. Senator Ervin's opening statement set the stage for the historical occasion:

If the allegations that have been made in the wake of the Watergate affair are substantiated, there has been a very serious subversion of the integrity of the electoral process, and the committee will be obliged to consider the manner in which such a subversion affects the continued existence of this Nation as a representative democracy, and how, if we are to survive, such subversions may be prevented in the future.[50]

Television covered the opening day and every day thereafter of the Watergate hearings, gavel-to-gavel, until August 7. The commercial networks logged a total of 319 hours of coverage during the period at an estimated cost of some $10 million.[51] During that time, officials from the Nixon administration and the Committee for the Re-election of the President "unfolded tales of big money, dirty tricks, taping of presidential conversations and possible law violations."[52]

Full coverage by the three commercial networks continued for the first five days (averaging about five hours per day) of the hearings. By June 5, however, the networks had devised a rotation plan that shifted coverage responsibility from one network to another every third day.[53] The rotation agreement allowed any network to cover as much of the hearing as it wanted, regardless of its primary coverage responsibility on a particular day. As it happened, the three networks elected to carry simultaneous coverage on only one occasion after June 5—during the testimony of former White House counsel John Dean. His testimony alone consumed nearly thirty hours.

While commercial television aired the Watergate hearings live, the Public Broadcasting Service (PBS) carried them on a taped, delayed basis during the evening. These delayed telecasts proved extraordinarily beneficial to public broadcasting. Cash contributions to local PBS stations airing the hearings increased dramatically,[54] as did program ratings, which, for public television, were usually abysmally low during the evening. Many public television station managers were at first reluctant to air the hearings in view of their stations' dependence on federal funds for operating expenses. But public demand grew to such an extent that 92 percent of the stations eventually were carrying the hearings. According to one commentator, "Watergate was probably the most important thing that has happened to noncommercial public affairs reporting since its founding."[55]

As phase one of the hearings ended on August 7, hearing viewership had declined slightly. Nonetheless, a Gallup Poll conducted during the first week of August indicated a substantial 58 percent of the public preferred that the hearings continue to be televised.[56] That would not be the case, though; when the Ervin Committee resumed its hearings on September 24, full-time television coverage did not return.[57]

Several senators had demanded that television cameras be removed from the hearing room before the committee had concluded its initial phase. To that end, Sen. Robert Dole (R-Kans.) introduced S.Res. 164 (later revised to S.Res. 166) on September 5. Arguing that "Congress cannot afford—and the public will not tolerate—an unending and all-consuming preoccupation with Watergate," Dole's unsuccessful resolution would have allowed continued broadcast coverage of the Watergate hearings but not on a live basis.[58]

The Ervin Committee extended public hearings through February 19, 1974, when it voted to conclude its work in executive sessions. Subsequently, the Senate extended the life of the committee to May 28 to allow it enough time to complete a final report of its findings. When the Ervin Committee finally disbanded, much of what it had uncovered was already in the hands of the House Judiciary Committee, whose job it would be to consider whether such findings constituted impeachable offenses.[59]

Public interest in the televised Watergate hearings was impressive. One survey showed that 85 percent of U.S. households had tuned in to some portion of the hearings.[60] An audience in 47.4 million homes viewed the hearings during their first week, and, throughout the duration of the Watergate hearings, most Americans relied on television for information about the proceedings.[61]

Televised Hearings Challenged

The previous chapter noted many of the issues surrounding televised congressional hearings, particularly in regard to television's impact on the due process rights of a hearing witness. One aspect of the due process issue not explored was the danger that if a witness, after testifying before a televised hearing, were later indicted, a court might rule any subsequent fair trial impossible because of pre-trial publicity resulting from the telecast. Prosecutors have made the point that quite often the government, and thus the public, are the ones with much to lose if a defendant can prove the impossibility of a fair trial. It was for this reason that the Ervin Committee's use of television was challenged.

The first challenge came on June 4, when Special Prosecutor Archibald Cox urged Senator Ervin to postpone his committee's hearings from one to three months. Referring to the effect that television cameras might have on testimony before the Watergate panel, Cox argued that the "continuation of hearings . . . would create grave danger that the full facts about the Watergate case and related matters will never come to light and that many of those who are guilty of serious wrong-doing will never be brought to justice." Members of the Ervin Committee met in executive session on June 5 to consider the Cox request and voted to reject it.[62] When the hearings reconvened later in the same day, Senator Ervin announced the committee's decision and remarked that the importance in continuing the proceedings on a televised basis lay in the opportunity for the American public to learn the full facts of Watergate.[63]

The committee's reply did not stop Prosecutor Cox from filing a motion before U.S. District Judge John Sirica on June 6, asking that the committee hear the testimony of two key Watergate witnesses—Jeb Magruder and John Dean—in executive session. Again, Cox was concerned with the possibility that pretrial publicity would harm chances for "bringing to justice those guilty of serious offenses in high government offices." Cox was referring both to the effect on future trials of Magruder and Dean and to trials of persons who might be implicated in criminal activity by testimony from the two. The Ervin Committee promptly answered Cox's motion by filing a brief with Judge Sirica insisting that the separation of powers doctrine gave the court no jurisdiction over the committee's action.[64] Sirica, agreeing with the committee, dismissed Cox's motion. "In hindsight," remarked one observer, "perhaps even Cox would agree that the televised testimony of Dean and Magruder produced far more good than harm. It was the testimony of these two men that first helped the nation understand the extent of the Watergate affair."[65]

A third attempt to enjoin the televised hearings was made by Rabbi Baruch Korff, an ardent defender of President Nixon. Rabbi Korff charged that the committee conducted its proceedings with "considerable attendant theatrics" and "histrionic questioning" and that it had "deliberately and inequitably disrupted the domestic tranquility of the United States."[66] District Judge June Green dismissed Korff's suit, and later attempts to appeal the decision proved equally unsuccessful.[67]

The last word on the matter remained with the Ervin Committee. In its final report the committee gave the following assessment of television's role during the Watergate hearings:

The committee's interest in televised hearings was not to obtain publicity for publicity's sake. The facts which the committee produced dealt with the very integrity of the electoral process; they were facts, the committee believed, the public had a right to know. Most citizens are not able personally to attend the working sessions of their Government. Although thousands of people spent short periods in the Caucus Room during the hearings, these visitors represented only a small percentage of the electorate. Thus, it was desirable that every citizen be able to view the hearings, if not in the Caucus Room, then in his home or place of business. The ability to read about the hearings in the printed media was not sufficient. The full import of the hearings could only be achieved by observing the witnesses and hearing their testimony.[68]

TELEVISED IMPEACHMENT PROCEEDINGS

On February 6, 1974, the House passed H.Res. 803 by a vote of 410 to 4, authorizing its Judiciary Committee

to investigate fully and completely whether sufficient grounds exist for the House of Representatives to exercise its constitutional power to impeach Richard M. Nixon, President of the United States of America. The Committee shall report to the House of Representatives such resolutions, articles of impeachment, or other recommendations as it deems proper.

From late February until mid-July, the Judiciary Committee gathered and studied documents and conducted hearings relative to establishing a case against the President. Once the investigatory phase of its deliberations had ended, the committee scheduled open meetings for July 24, 25, 26, 27, 29 and 30 to debate what recommendations it would make to the House. Three articles were eventually adopted by the Judiciary Committee recommending that the House move ahead to initiate impeachment proceedings against President Nixon.[69]

The six days of committee debate were televised in their entirety. Realizing that impeachment proceedings might progress to the committee stage, during the first half of 1974 several representatives had introduced resolutions to allow their being telecast. The last to be introduced was Rep. Wayne Owens' (D-Utah) H.Res. 1107.[70] The resolution was referred to the Rules Committee and then reported favorably to the House on July 18.[71]

The full House considered H.Res. 1107 during a brief debate on July 22. Rep. John Anderson (R-Ill.) opposed opening Judiciary Committee deliberations to television at what he considered too late a date. He felt that by showing the "final leg of the inquiry" viewers might get the impression that members of the committee had not given sufficient consideration to all the evidence that had come before them. Absent from view would be the agonized shifting of opinion as they weighed item after item of the evidence.

Rep. Robert Drinan (D-Mass.) opposed televising the deliberations on purely legal terms. He asserted that the proceedings were "quasi judicial" and therefore should be governed by the American Bar Association's ethics code which barred television and radio from American courtrooms. Moreover, he feared that prejudicial publicity resulting from the committee telecasts would deprive certain individuals from any chance of receiving fair trials.

It remained for Rep. Herman Badillo (D-N.Y.) to present the most compelling argument in support of televising the Judiciary Committee's deliberations:

If it is true that great numbers of Americans are losing faith in the institutions of government because of the catalog of improper activities being revealed daily through the courts, congressional committees, and the press, then I believe that we have an obligation to attempt to use the impeachment debate as a mechanism to get the American people involved in a public dialogue and also to demonstrate to them that the system, for all its imperfections and procrastination, is operating in a climate of civility, reason, and due process.

House Resolution 1107 was approved overwhelmingly by a vote of 346 to 40.[72]

Although the full House had cleared the way, the Judiciary Committee still had to vote on whether to allow television to cover its proceedings. Shortly after the House vote, the committee gave its approval by a substantial 31 to 7 margin. One major concession required of network television was that no commercial interruptions be allowed while the committee was in session.[73]

The Judiciary Committee convened its televised deliberations on the evening of July 24. Network coverage was arranged on the same rotational basis as had been used to cover the Senate Watergate hearings.[74] But, whereas the commercial networks chose to cover only the evening sessions of the debates, PBS offered its non-commercial television affiliates telecasts of the morning and afternoon sessions as well—providing some thirteen hours of coverage per day during the entire six days of open deliberations.[75]

Praise for the conduct of Judiciary Committee members and for television's role in covering the committee's proceedings was nearly unanimous in the American press. As an example, the following appeared in the *New York Times*:

> After four full days of coverage, the verdict is clear. The decision to televise the House Judiciary Committee debates . . . is fully justified. While the presence of TV cameras has undoubtedly had some effect on the participants, that effect has often been positive, keeping blatant or excessive posturing to a bearable minimum. Meantime, the public is afforded invaluable access to, and understanding of, a historical event.[76]

A sharp increase in public approval of Congress in general was attributed by the Gallup Poll to the Judiciary Committee's "thorough and judicious" television appearance. A poll report released on August 29 showed a 48 percent approval rating,[77] up some 18 percentage points from only four months earlier.[78]

JOINT COMMITTEE ON CONGRESSIONAL OPERATIONS

Nestled between the activity of the Senate's Ervin Committee and the House Judiciary Committee were the hearings of the Joint Committee on Congressional Operations. Sen. Lee Metcalf (D-Mont.), committee co-chairman, announced in December 1973 that the committee would open public hearings on

February 20, 1974, on the subject of "Congress and mass communications." "During these hearings," stated Metcalf, "we will examine the growing imbalance between the capabilities of the Congress and the Executive to reach the American people through the mass communications media." The committee would invite opinions from a number of sources on how Congress could better explain its constitutional role as an institution and its day-to-day operation. The hearings would follow closely in the wake of a study recently released by the Senate Subcommittee on Intergovernmental Relations (see Chapter 1) showing that the deterioration of congressional communication with the public could no longer be ignored.[79]

The CRS Study

Prior to its hearings the committee had requested that the Congressional Research Service (CRS) prepare a background study that would "suggest and evaluate various ways that Congress might more effectively communicate the meaning of its constitutional role and daily activities to the American people."[80] Several methods of achieving that objective were examined by the CRS, but only one was advocated as having the greatest potential for effectively showing Congress at work: live telecasts of House and Senate chamber proceedings. Examples of successful legislative assembly broadcasts from several other countries were cited as proof that the U.S. Congress could achieve similar success.[81]

If the joint committee agreed with the CRS assessment, two controversial and potentially divisive problems would have to be resolved: first, what coverage method would be most appropriate; second, who would manage the coverage system? The CRS study addressed both problems, presenting advantages and disadvantages to alternative solutions for each.

As for coverage method, two were described as having the greatest potential. One would allow television to cover the closing moments of debate on major legislation when arguments from both sides of a matter under consideration are summarized. The other would open the floor to televised coverage at all times. By doing the latter it was felt that once television cameras blended into the surroundings the likelihood of congressmen playing to them would diminish. However, even this method had its disadvantages: Constant television coverage was seen as possibly altering the nature of floor debates in unpredictable ways that might not prove beneficial to Congress. In addition, since it would be doubtful that network television would air great quantities of often routine and uninteresting floor activity, viewers would continue to receive little information about Congress.[82]

What proceedings would or would not be covered rested squarely on who would be managing the coverage system. The networks (both commercial and non-commercial) could provide pool coverage facilities in the House and Senate chambers, but a network-managed system meant a system independent of congressional control. Another possible management system might be based on that at the United Nations. A "congressional television and radio service" would be organized to provide audio and video feeds to whomever might subscribe to them, would record all proceedings, would supply taped excerpts by special request to local stations and would provide closed-circuit radio/television feeds to congressional offices. Disadvantages in this approach would be censorship and propaganda allegations from journalists and possible refusals by network technicians to air any taped or live coverage originated by non-union employees. A third approach would require the creation of a quasi-public corporation to manage a system that would function in much the same fashion as the congressional television and radio service described above. This approach would eliminate problems posed by full congressional control or by full network control. The corporation would be non-profit but would generate enough funds to maintain itself by subscriber fees for its service. A fourth approach would contain all the elements of the third but would establish a special Library of Congress unit to manage the coverage system.

The CRS study emphasized that these were only suggestions and that variations and combinations of elements contained in each might yield the most suitable management system. A trial period on a closed-circuit basis for whatever system Congress might choose would allow time to experiment and to perfect the system before making coverage available to the public.[83]

Joint Committee Hearings

Six days of hearings before the Joint Committee on Congressional Operations began on February 20, 1974, and continued at periodic intervals through April 10. Committee Chairman Metcalf laid the foundation for the hearings by asserting that Congress's weak public image resulted from its correspondingly weak ability to communicate with the public:

A Congress unable to project its voice much beyond the banks of the Potomac—to be heard and understood only dimly outside Washington, D.C.—can be neither representative nor responsive. A Congress able only to whisper, no matter how intelligently, cannot check and balance the power of the Executive or safeguard the liberty of the individual citizen.[84]

Sen. Edmund Muskie (D-Maine) echoed Chairman Metcalf's sentiments. He had chaired the Subcommittee on Intergovernmental Relations, whose report showed public attitudes toward Congress to be at a discouraging level. Muskie suggested that better congressional information flow would improve public perception of the institution, but he opposed relying on the press. Rather, Muskie favored "finding new ways to inform the people directly, without intermediaries." "Obviously," he remarked, "television is the only medium that can carry such a message for us effectively."[85]

Joint Committee Vice Chairman Rep. Jack Brooks (D-Tex.) was not as optimistic as Senator Muskie. He felt that televising congressional chamber proceedings was not the ideal approach. Instead of increasing public understanding of Congress, televised chamber proceedings would add to the confusion, in Brooks's view. "Gavel-to-gavel coverage of the proceedings," as he described it, "would be similar to continuous coverage of hospital operating rooms for the purpose of improving the image and understanding of the medical profession."[86]

Presidents and news personnel of the three commercial television networks defended both the amount and the quality of their congressional coverage. Committee members could hardly agree with that assessment and argued that network news reports of congressional activity were oftentimes insufficient and unfair. The network representatives countered that Congress was to blame for what it regarded as poor coverage, since Congress had mandated procedural restrictions that continued to hamper proper television news access to the Capitol and congressional office buildings. A more accommodating Congress, contended the network representatives, would result in more and better congressional coverage.[87]

Former CBS News President Fred Friendly, whose disagreement with that network was described earlier, cautioned the committee to be skeptical of network intentions: "Perhaps my battle scars show, but I should not be optimistic about any increase in the quality of congressional coverage in network prime time, nor do I believe that the commercial daytime schedule will permit much congressional coverage to interfere with the schedule of soap operas and game shows."[88]

Many congressmen remained concerned that television's presence would adversely affect congressional proceedings, but committee testimony about state legislatures whose deliberative proceedings had been covered by television showed the experience to have been a beneficial one. S. Anders Yokom of the Connecticut Educational Television Corporation said that legislators became slightly long-winded and attempted some "showboating" when television first was allowed on the Connecticut legislature's floor, but that kind of behavior soon subsided.[89] And Fred Rebman of WJCT-TV in Jacksonville, Florida, provided the committee with studies showing that televised coverage of the Florida state legislature at times had attracted a greater audience than some popular network talk shows, had improved public understanding of the legislature, had increased public feedback to legislators on particular issues, and had made legislators more attentive to their duties.[90]

The final hearing day moved the joint committee from a discussion of philosophical and procedural matters to a discussion of technology. It so happened that coinciding with the committee's investigation of methods to improve congressional communication was a revolution in the telecommunications industry. Components of that revolution would enable Congress (if it availed itself of the opportunity) to utilize television in ways unimagined only a few years earlier.

Cable television and communications satellites offered Congress the greatest communications potential. Traditional broadcast networks and stations could be circumvented by transporting congressional telecasts via satellite to local cable systems throughout the country. Cable television's "narrowcasting" capabilities would provide Congress with even greater possibilities. Narrowcasting would enable cable systems with their multiple channel capacity to carry several congressional events simultaneously.[91]

Several conclusions may be drawn from the joint committee hearings. First, testimony had shown, as the committee would state in its interim report, that

1) The potential for bringing more information about congressional activities directly to more Americans through broadcast coverage of activities in the House and Senate chambers is substantial;
2) The experience of other legislatures which have permitted such coverage under varying conditions over the past several years has been generally favorable; and
3) The technology of communications is sufficiently advanced to provide for televising or recording unobtrusively without disrupting floor proceedings.[92]

A second conclusion is that most congressmen shared a distrust for television news and a displeasure in the way television reporters covered congressional activities. Arguments by network representatives that their news organizations did a good job of covering Congress were not convincing. Committee members were inclined to trace much of Congress's poor public image to the disrespectful manner in which the networks portrayed it.

A third conclusion is that television news representatives placed little trust in Congress's controlling television access to its floor proceedings. "Censorship" and "propaganda" were the terms most commonly applied. The only kind of coverage supported by all the media was that which would provide free and total access to all congressional activity.

Joint Committee Interim Report

The joint committee issued an interim report of its findings and recommendations on October 10, 1974. The committee expressed its support for daily, gavel-to-gavel televised coverage of congressional floor proceedings, and it recommended that the telecasts be made available to House offices via closed circuit and videotaped for research purposes and distribution to educational institutions. As expected, the committee felt that "adaptation of the [television] system in operation at the United Nations would be most likely to realize the potential of broadcasting—including communications *within* Congress—with the least likelihood of undesirable side effects." But the committee felt that the expense of implementing a television system required, as a first step, "a carefully designed but limited test to determine the ultimate feasibility and desirability of a permanent system for broadcasting activities in the House and Senate Chambers."

The report provided two recommendations for conducting the test: 1) a closed-circuit *video* feed to certain House and Senate offices that would be available to broadcasters following a sixty-day technical "shakedown" period; and 2) a closed-circuit *audio* feed carried to each congressional office via existing telephone lines and available to broadcasters after a thirty-day "shakedown" period. The report recommended that the test begin early in the Ninety-fourth Congress and that it be under the direction of either the joint committee, the House and Senate Rules Committees or an ad hoc committee. The Public Broadcasting Service was recommended as the logical technical entity to conduct the closed-circuit test and to originate the eventual broadcasts.

Additional recommendations were that modern, light-sensitive cameras be used; that the cameras be stationed in the galleries, not on the floors of either house; that only cameras from the entity chosen to conduct the test be allowed inside the congressional chambers; that enough cameras be used so as not to require House and Senate members to speak from unaccustomed locations; that "panning" and "reaction" shots be prohibited; that procedures be adopted "to ensure that broadcast coverage is carried out in a non-partisan manner and is fair and equitable in recording the views of Members participating in floor proceedings"; and that a mechanism be created whereby members of Congress may voice grievances pertaining to congressional television and radio floor coverage. Comprehensive evaluations would accompany each phase of the test. Finally, the report recommended that rules be enacted to prohibit use of live or recorded broadcast floor proceedings in commercial messages and in political campaign announcements and programs.[93]

Although it would not be released for nearly a year, the joint committee's final report reiterated the recommendations in its interim report. The final report also called for reorganizing the press gallery to better accommodate the electronic and the print media and a review by appropriate authorities of the complicated regulations governing use of broadcast equipment to record interviews in or near the U.S. Capitol Building.[94]

Two months after release of the committee's interim report, Sen. Lee Metcalf incorporated its recommendations into S.Res. 447.[95] The resolution had minimal chance of success, since the Ninety-third Congress adjourned shortly after the measure's introduction. Though its days were numbered, S.Res. 447 was a precursor of later legislative efforts, all of which would trace their origin to the work of the Joint Committee on Congressional Operations.

LIVE TELEVISION FROM THE SENATE

As a postscript to the increased attention being paid congressional television during this period, the U.S. Senate invited television cameras into its chamber on December 19, 1974, to cover the swearing-in ceremony of Vice President Nelson Rockefeller. The historical significance of the event was twofold: Rockefeller was the second U.S. Vice President in less than a year to be appointed rather than elected to office, and television cameras covering his swearing in were the first ever allowed inside the Senate chamber. All three commercial television networks aired the brief fifteen-minute ceremony.[96] The way had been cleared for televising the event by Senate passage of S.Res. 452 on December 14. The measure, introduced by Sen. Robert Byrd (D-W.Va.), restricted coverage to the single occasion and won Senate approval without debate.

5 · Congress Considers Chamber Television

During the Ninety-fourth and Ninety-fifth Congresses, the issue of congressional television took independent courses in the House and in the Senate. Both houses approached the matter on quite different terms and both exhibited a different degree of urgency as they studied implementation methods.

TELEVISION IN THE SENATE, NINETY-FOURTH CONGRESS

On January 28, 1975, Sen. Lee Metcalf reintroduced his resolution from the previous Congress, providing for a test of closed-circuit television from the Senate chamber. The new resolution, S.Res. 39, was identical to its predecessor. Although co-sponsored by one-third of the Senate, including Majority Leader Mike Mansfield and Minority Leader Hugh Scott (R-Pa.),[1] S.Res. 39 received no action during the remainder of the Ninety-fourth Congress.

An alternate route for implementing Senate television seemed in the making when Sen. James McClure (R-Idaho) introduced a resolution in June 1975 to provide for televised coverage of debate on the contested New Hampshire senatorial election. The dispute over whether Republican Louis Wyman or Democrat John Durkin had won election would have to be settled by the

Senate. Anticipating the wide interest that debate on the subject might generate, Senator McClure introduced S.Res. 177 to allow for televising the proceedings.

Majority Leader Mansfield enthusiastically supported the McClure Resolution, calling it "a suggestion whose time has come." Majority Whip Robert Byrd was no less enthusiastic in his support, but he wondered how interested the networks might be. Byrd felt that long hours of the Senate's traditionally unlimited debate would not attract gavel-to-gavel coverage. And if the networks did elect to cover debate, Byrd worried that senators might "string out" their speeches even more than usual as they played to the television audience. That possibility compelled him to offer an amendment to S.Res. 177 that would make televising the Wyman-Durkin debate "contingent upon some limitation of debate being ordered by the Senate." In other words, unless the Senate gave its unanimous consent to hold individual arguments to certain prearranged time limits, television would not be allowed.[2] Byrd's amendment was approved and immediately thereafter so was S.Res. 177.[3]

Though things seemed settled procedurally, there remained a technical impasse. Network representatives insisted on using more cameras than the Senate would allow and on increasing the Senate chamber's light level.[4] Senate representatives opposed adding extra lights due to the load the light-generated heat would put on the air-conditioning system, not to mention the glare and "artificial environment" that would accompany the extra lights.[5] Unfortunately, the lighting problem would not be resolved by the time the Wyman-Durkin debate began.[6]

Interest in Senate chamber television declined following Wyman-Durkin. Not until release of a 1976 report by the Commission on the Operation of the Senate would that interest be revived. The commission, chaired by former Sen. Harold Hughes (D-Iowa), was especially interested in discovering methods by which the Senate could establish more direct lines of communication with the public. To aid in this endeavor the commission requested that several authorities prepare reports describing the present status of Senate communication practices and wherever possible to recommend ways of improving those practices.[7] One of the key reports, prepared by former NBC News executive Len Allen, was entitled "Television from the Senate Floor."

Allen's opening statement cut squarely to the heart of the matter: "The Senate should end its long-standing ban on broadcast coverage of its floor activity as a means of sharpening public awareness of the co-equal role of Congress in the American political system."[8] The report went on to outline specific procedures that the Senate might follow to implement televised floor coverage.[9]

The commission endorsed Allen's assessment and in its final report emphasized the importance of the Senate chamber as the "institution's center stage" ("It is here that Senate debate and decisionmaking are seen in full force. It is here, finally and formally, that views are delineated, ideas are challenged, courses of action are defended, and agreements and compromises are realized," read the report) and therefore recommended that the Senate "conduct a full-scale experiment of audio and video broadcasting of floor proceedings." The implementation stages and eventual broadcast system characteristics it outlined[10] were almost identical to those prescribed in the Metcalf Resolution then pending before the Senate.

TELEVISION IN THE HOUSE, NINETY-FOURTH CONGRESS

Rep. John Anderson initiated House efforts in the Ninety-fourth Congress to implement the recommendations of the Joint Committee on Congressional Operations. Anderson's H.Res. 110, introduced on January 29, 1975, was a lean measure simply authorizing the Speaker of the House to conduct a test of audio and video coverage of House proceedings, after which time he should make coverage signals available to broadcasters.

A more substantive measure, H.Res. 269, was introduced a month later by Rep. Jack Brooks. The Brooks Resolution was identical (save for minor technical alterations) to the one Senator Metcalf had introduced in the Senate. The House Rules Committee scheduled hearings on the measure in mid-April.[11]

During the first day of hearings, several House members voiced their continued concern that the House chamber would become a "circus" or even a "burlesque" if television cameras were admitted. Others were displeased that, regardless of who originated the telecast, the ultimate decision of what home viewers would see of Congress would be made by broadcasters. They believed that once the television signal carrying congressional proceedings came into the hands of the broadcasters, it would be edited to the point of distorting its content.[12]

Following its April 16 session, the Rules Committee conducted one more set of hearings before sending H.Res. 269 to a special subcommittee headed by Rep. B. F. Sisk.

It is of particular significance that Representative Sisk was named to chair the Ad Hoc Subcommittee on Broadcasting. Sisk was a twenty-year veteran of Congress[13] who had distinguished himself as manager of the House bill (H.R. 17654) that became the 1970 Legislative Reorganization Act. Though never identified as a congressional reformer, Representative Sisk was respected among his colleagues for his fairness and his tenaciousness.[14] In view of his efforts toward passage of the law that opened House committee proceedings to television, it could be assumed that Sisk maintained a favorable attitude toward televising House chamber proceedings.

Besides Sisk, five others were appointed to the subcommittee: Representatives John Anderson, Claude Pepper, Morgan Murphy (D-Ill.), Andrew Young (D-Ga.), and Delwin Clawson (R-Calif.). Representatives Anderson and Pepper were the subcommittee's two known quantities. Pepper's advocacy of House television was legendary; Anderson was on record as supporting House television and would emerge as perhaps the most vocal defender of the subcommittee's eventual proposals. Though their positions were unknown, Representatives Young's and Murphy's liberal voting record[15] suggested advocacy for House television, while Representative Clawson's conservative record[16] suggested opposition.

As it began its task, the subcommittee appeared aided by the generally supportive attitude of House members toward chamber television. There was also a congressional reform effort under way that seemed to be carrying prospects for House television with it. But, when all seemed poised for quick action on the Brooks proposal, there were those who warned that such would not be the case. As one former House employee observed, "Members by and large are leery of taking a risk that they cannot step back from."[17]

The Sisk Subcommittee invited representatives from the four television networks (NBC, CBS, ABC and PBS) to conduct a television feasibility study of the House chamber in September 1975. The network group determined that the present light level was too low for quality television pictures but that new light fixtures soon to be installed would bring the level up to a suitable fifty foot candles; moreover, television cameras could be situated in existing doorways leading to the House visitors' gallery so that only the camera lenses would be visible from inside the chamber. The network group also said that a minimum of four cameras would be needed to allow for optimum shots of speakers standing at the two podiums in the well of the House and at the Speaker's rostrum.

Based on the study's results, the networks proposed that they be allowed to televise House proceedings on a one-year trial basis. A network pool would be arranged to furnish equipment and personnel to televise the proceedings on a gavel-to-gavel basis. The networks would use excerpts from live video and audio feeds for their newscasts and in turn would sell the continuous feed to the House for whatever purposes the House might choose. It was proposed that the Sisk Subcommittee submit a resolution incorporating the plan so that the broadcasts could begin by January.[18]

While H.Res. 269 was still pending, the subcommittee accommodated the networks by introducing H.Res. 875 on November 19. The resolution's provisions closely paralleled those proposed by the networks. Other H.Res. 875 (or network plan) provisions were similar to those of H.Res. 269 (the Brooks plan). Both allowed unlimited selection of House coverage material for broadcast use but stressed that such material be used only for the "education, enlightenment and information of the general public." Both prohibited commercial sponsorship of House broadcasts (live or recorded) and both prohibited use of recorded House broadcasts for political campaign purposes.

The plans had two major dissimilarities. Whereas the Brooks plan designated the House Commission on Information and Facilities to manage the House broadcasting system, the network plan contained no management provisions. And while the Information and Facilities Commission was given jurisdiction over recording and storing videotapes of House proceedings under the

Brooks plan, that job would belong to the Library of Congress under the network plan.[19]

The Sisk Subcommittee preference for the network plan soon became apparent. That preference became more obvious in early December when the subcommittee scheduled two days of hearings on the measure. Testimony from Representative Brooks showed him to be understandably resentful over the treatment of his resolution. What is more, his opposition to the network plan was stated in precise terms: first, the plan failed to provide a non-broadcast test period; second, it failed to provide for a supervisory authority to oversee and formulate rules; third, it granted a monopoly over the sale and distribution of House proceedings coverage to the four networks; and fourth, it elevated the networks' commercial interests above the interests of Congress. Regarding the final point, Brooks stressed that "the fundamental purpose of opening Congressional proceedings to a wider public must be to perform a public service—a service that emphasizes the interest of the people and their institutions rather than those of the media, themselves."[20]

The Sisk Subcommittee remained unswayed and met twice more following its two days of hearings to refine H.Res. 875. During meetings on December 11, 1975, and February 4, 1976, subcommittee members adopted several "perfecting amendments" to the resolution.[21] One prohibited any entity under contract to broadcast House floor proceedings from obtaining a copyright on recordings of those proceedings. The major amendment, though, was in response to Representative Brooks's criticism of the absence of any supervisory body to oversee operation of the coverage system prescribed in the network plan. The subcommittee answered the criticism by inserting the following new provision: "There shall be established within the Committee on Rules in each Congress a Broadcast Advisory Board to be appointed by the chairman for the purpose of assisting the Committee in its responsibilities to supervise, review, study, and coordinate, on a continuing basis, the television and radio coverage of the proceedings of the House."[22]

The subcommittee then voted to recommend that the House Rules Committee support H.Res. 875 in its amended form. The vote was delayed when House Speaker Carl Albert (D-Okla.) sent word that he objected to the subcommittee usurping his prerogatives by naming a Broadcast Advisory Board to perform functions that conflicted with his traditional control of the House chamber. The subcommittee noted the Speaker's protest but still decided against deleting the advisory board provision.[23]

The subcommittee's action was ill-advised. Speaker Albert insisted that his control of the House chamber was absolute and that subcommittee members would be wise to reconsider their positions. So that the full cooperation of the subcommittee might be demonstrated, all of its members met with the Speaker and with House Majority Leader "Tip" O'Neill (D-Mass.) on February 24 to settle their differences. An excerpt from the report of that meeting provides a glimpse of the amelioratory approach taken by the Sisk Subcommittee to win the House leadership's support for H.Res. 875:

Since it has never been the intention of the Subcommittee to in any way detract from the Speaker's control over the Chamber which is clearly spelled out in clause 3, rule I of the Rules of the House of Representatives, the Subcommittee agreed to draft amendatory language to the resolution which would explicitly reaffirm the prerogatives of the Speaker in this area.

Several meetings followed with members of the Speaker's and the subcommittee's staffs drafting final language for the necessary amendments. Once the work was completed, the subcommittee met on March 4, and again voted to report H.Res. 875 to the Rules Committee. The resolution's new version contained three essential changes: 1) responsibility that originally had been vested in the Clerk of the House, with the approval of the Rules Committee, for entering into contracts and for making necessary arrangements for House broadcast coverage now would be vested in the Speaker; 2) jurisdiction over the Broadcast Advisory Board would move from the Rules Committee to the Speaker, with ultimate decision-making powers over matters coming before the board resting solely with the Speaker; and 3) deletion of all references to a network pool arrangement, since such a provision allowing for the Clerk of the House to "enter into a contract with a particular private party" was unprecedented in the Speaker's view.[24]

The amended version of H. Res. 875 now on the Rules Committee agenda still was destined for opposition from House Speaker Albert and Majority Leader O'Neill, even after the Sisk Subcommittee had acceded to the Speaker's demands. In fact, a subcommittee staff member surmised that Albert and O'Neill were "shocked" when the subcommittee met the demands. "They thought they'd be major items with us and that a compromise would break down over those issues," said the staff member. Rules Committee Chairman Madden postponed several committee meetings to consider H. Res. 875, presumably at the request of Albert and O'Neill, before finally scheduling a meeting on March 24. Once the date had been set, one Rules Committee member said that Majority Leader O'Neill had asked Chairman Sisk not to bring H. Res. 875 to the floor for discussion. Although O'Neill's opposition to the resolution was not acknowledged by either him or his aides, the Majority Leader's strategy obviously was directed toward preventing H. Res. 875 from reaching the floor.[25]

The Rules Committee met as scheduled to debate H. Res. 875. Almost from the moment the meeting came to order, the prevailing majority attitudes signaled trouble for the measure. Chairman Ray Madden, an acknowledged opponent of House television, led the assault. He claimed that members would be standing in line waiting to speak in the House chamber if television coverage were introduced during the current election year. Rep. Richard Bolling (D-Mo.) was displeased with the Sisk Subcommittee's having presented the Rules Committee with only one coverage system to choose from. He suggested that the committee as well as the entire House should have the benefit of choosing from among several possible systems.[26]

The few favorable comments came from members of the Sisk Subcommittee. Representative Anderson said that nearly every one of the resolution's provisions had received bipartisan support during subcommittee deliberations.[27] He also insisted that "obstructionist or delaying tactics" should not be employed against H. Res. 875 at the Rules Committee stage; rather, the measure should be reported to the floor so that the full House could judge its merits and decide its fate.[28]

However, H. Res. 875 was not destined to reach the House floor. As the Rules Committee meeting drew to a close, its members voted 9 to 7 in favor of a motion by Rep. John Young (D-Tex.) to recommit the resolution, thus sending it back to the Sisk Subcommittee. Representative Young said that it was not his intent to kill the measure, only to induce more study.[29] Intentions notwithstanding, his motion struck a near fatal blow to H.Res. 875.

Representative Sisk was reluctant to admit defeat. In early April he wrote a letter to all subcommittee members explaining his intentions to make one additional attempt before the end of the Ninety-fourth Congress to resurrect H.Res. 875 in yet another version of its original. He already had instructed his subcommittee staff to begin collecting material on alternative coverage plans so that appropriate implementation amendments to H.Res. 875 could be made.[30] If Congress wanted a "multiple choice" resolution, as Representative Anderson suggested, then the Sisk Subcommittee would supply it.

Meanwhile, Representative Pepper released a report on a poll he had conducted in mid-May to ascertain House member attitudes toward House broadcast coverage and particular coverage systems. Of the 346 questionnaire respondents, 238 (69 percent) favored radio and television coverage. Fifty-nine percent of those favoring television said they would support a network pool system. Forty-seven percent would support a system operated by the Public Broadcasting Service, but only 30 percent indicated support for a system operated by the House itself.[31]

On August 30, almost six months after the Sisk Subcommittee staff had resumed work on H.Res. 875, the subcommittee was prepared to reintroduce its resolution. Along with certain changes in the basic content the numerical designation also had changed from H.Res. 875 to H.Res. 1502. The most striking content change was the addition of a new clause stating, "It is the sense of the House that the initial television and radio coverage of the proceedings of the House should be provided by a pool arrangement with the American Broadcasting Company, CBS, Inc., the National Broadcasting Company, and the Public Broadcasting Service."[32]

The intent of the new clause was twofold: first, it returned language to the resolution that had been removed in March at Speaker Albert's request. But the subcommittee, rather than resorting to language that would have made implementation of a pool coverage system mandatory, instead used the "sense of the House" terminology that would have advised the Speaker of the members' coverage system preference while still leaving the final implementation decision to him. The second intent was to provide an interchangeable mechanism by which the House had the option of substituting language that would provide for one of two other television coverage systems—one controlled by PBS (or a similar public entity) or one controlled by the House itself. So, if the House agreed to allow telecasts by a network pool group, the above clause would remain unchanged. If a coverage system controlled by PBS were favored, the language following the word "provided" would be changed to read "through the facilities and personnel of the Public Broadcasting Service."[33] And if a House controlled system were chosen, the language would be changed to read "by the House in such manner and under such administrative structure as the Speaker may designate, consistent with the purposes of this resolution."[34] Though the structure appeared unorthodox, the intended purpose was to present House members with what the Sisk Subcommittee had decided were the three most practical television coverage system options.

The subcommittee's efforts were impressive, but its timing poor; the odds against H.Res. 1502 reaching the House were nearly insurmountable. There was little time left in the Ninety-fourth Congress to consider the measure, assuming, of course, that it could reach the House floor. Beyond the fact that members of Congress were anxious to wrap up legislative business and to begin their reelection campaigns, Rules Committee Chairman Madden remained steadfast in his opposition to House television.[35] Without his support, it was unlikely that H.Res. 1502 would ever be brought before the committee. The resolution finally died along with the efforts of the Sisk Subcommittee as Congress adjourned.

TELEVISION IN THE SENATE, NINETY-FIFTH CONGRESS

Congress often postpones acting on matters until the time is ripe. For Senate chamber television that time seemed to occur in fall 1977 as the Senate prepared to debate the controversial Panama Canal Treaty. The treaty (actually, several individual but related treaties), signed by President Carter and President Torrijos of the Republic of Panama on September 7, would return control of the canal from the United States to Panama, pending Senate ratification. Noting the significance of the ratification debate, Sen. Robert Byrd introduced S.Res. 268 authorizing its coverage by radio and television. Byrd accompanied the introduction by remarking that citizens must be fully informed of all details of the ratification process so that the collective public wisdom could guide the Senate in making a proper final decision.[36]

Senate Resolution 268 was referred to the Committee on Rules and Administration. Between early October 1977 and late January 1978, the committee staff discussed television possibilities by conferring with several groups, including representatives from the major television networks, the staff of the Architect of the Capitol and the Senate Radio and TV Gallery. Camera locations were agreed to, but the low light level in the Senate chamber presented a formidable obstacle to airing a network-quality picture. Several lighting schemes were tested to raise the level, but the glare and intense heat caused by each proved too impractical. The existing chamber audio system was not of the best quality either, but technicians said that sound enhancement devices could improve the audio quality to an acceptable network standard. Choosing the most acceptable coverage system presented yet another problem. A decision could not be reached on whether to allow coverage by a network pool, a commercial service operating under Senate direction or a system comprised of equipment and personnel from other government sources.

In the end, the Rules Committee decided that lighting could not be upgraded sufficiently to comply with network standards in time for the scheduled Senate debates. The committee, therefore, amended S.Res. 268 by removing any reference to television, leaving only the provision for radio coverage. The amended S.Res. 268 was reported to the full Senate on February 2, 1978,[37] where it was considered and passed on the same day.[38]

The Panama Canal Treaty debate began on February 8. National Public Radio, CBS and NBC were all present to cover it, though CBS and NBC aired only a brief portion. NPR was committed to airing the entire debate, gavel-to-gavel. NPR reporter Linda Wertheimer, stationed in the Senate gallery, interrupted debate only long enough to review particular portions of the proceedings and to identify the speakers. There were slight technical problems as senators forgot to activate or deactivate hand-held microphones or as they laid a "live" microphone on a desk and walked away from it while continuing to speak. But, generally, NPR technicians thought the audio "was as good as it could be, considering it originated from the Senate's own microphone system."[39]

A survey of radio listeners in New York, Los Angeles and Washington, D.C. following the first week of debate showed that NPR's coverage had attracted more than five times the network's normal listenership. In fact, public radio listenership in New York alone increased by nearly 800 percent.[40]

NPR's impressive coverage won accolades from several sources. A *Washington Post* editorial, in reference to arguments that microphones and cameras placed inside the congressional chambers would alter the nature of Senate (and House) proceedings, agreed that radio coverage of the Panama Canal Treaty debate had indeed changed what happens on the Senate floor. But, the *Post* declared, the change "weighs heavily *in favor* of broadcasting." "Far from encouraging showboating," the *Post* continued, "the microphones seemed to concentrate senatorial minds and create conditions conducive to a spirited exchange of opposing views." The editorial concluded by praising public radio for "doing a service not just to the public but to the Senate as well."[41]

Members of the Senate were no less complimentary. Senator Robert Byrd said, "National Public Radio has been able to provide coverage of Senate debates and action with sensitivity, with professionalism, with accuracy, and with great understanding." He added that radio coverage of the debate had enhanced the American public's understanding of the Senate. Senator Spark Matsunaga (D-Hawaii) related how, during a recent meeting with a group of Chicago businessmen, most of them remarked that they had been listening to the debates and had expressed hopes that debates on other matters would be broadcast.[42]

The radio experiment proved eminently successful, but once debate on the Panama Canal Treaty had concluded, broadcasting departed the Senate chamber without any standing invitation to return.

TELEVISION IN THE HOUSE, NINETY-FIFTH CONGRESS

While chamber television remained a minor issue in the Senate, the same was hardly true in the House. Televising floor proceedings became a prime topic in that body no more than two months into the Ninety-fifth Congress.

On March 2, the new Speaker of the House, Thomas "Tip" O'Neill, announced unexpectedly that the House, beginning Tuesday, March 15, would conduct a ninety-day live test of television coverage of its floor proceedings. Television transmissions would be on a closed circuit with reception possible only in offices located in the Capitol and Rayburn House Office Building. The test would evaluate the feasibility of using small remote controlled cameras (only monochrome cameras at first), the usefulness of floor coverage as an information resource in House members' offices, and the historical value of preserving House proceedings on videotape. Speaker O'Neill said that the ninety-day test would form the basis for eventual public dissemination of televised House proceedings. He asserted that it would be mandatory for the House to maintain control of its evolving television system "to assure that any disturbance to the nature and character of the House proceedings be minimized and that any adjustments or accommodations be made in the selection and use of the technical equipment rather than to the existing proceedings of the House."[43]

The manner in which the ninety-day test was announced—its suddenness, especially—caught supporters of House television off guard. Rep. John Anderson finally responded a few days later, criticizing the Speaker for operating "out of the hip pocket" in conducting a test that had "not been developed by any standing committee of the House" nor "debated or authorized by the full House." Anderson followed his remarks by introducing a revised version of the resolution that the Sisk Subcommittee had promoted so doggedly during the preceding Congress. The major change in the new H.Res. 181 was the absence of any recommended coverage control system. The control decision wisely would be left in the hands of the Speaker.[44]

The ninety-day test began inauspiciously on March 15. Three cameras, focused on key locations in the House chamber, were operated from a remote control panel located in the visitors' gallery. Few House members were identifiable on television monitors due to a minimum of close-up shots. Since viewing was limited to a monitor in the Rayburn Room, just off the House floor, and a few monitors in the Rayburn House Office Building, very few watched the proceedings. One observer, unawed by the occasion, said watching the floor activity "certainly beat monitoring the lobby of a retirement hotel after midnight. . . . But not by much."[45]

Regardless of their on-camera appearance, House members present on the floor during the inaugural closed-circuit telecast were nearly unanimous in their praise for Speaker O'Neill's role in implementing the ninety-day test. Even Representative Anderson's critical demeanor had subsided as he too joined in praising the Speaker and the historical moment. Anderson concluded by introducing a resolution (H.Res. 404) authorizing "an evaluation by the Committee on Rules which would, at the conclusion of the [ninety-day] test, report back its findings and recommendations to the House, including a recommendation as to whether this coverage should be made available to the public through normal broadcast channels." The resolution was approved by a 398 to 10 vote.[46]

Management of the ninety-day test was placed under the authority of the Select (formerly Joint) Committee on Congressional Operations. Technical assistance to the committee was supplied by the Architect of the Capitol and the House Recording Studio. The Architect supplied camera operators and maintained the cable or Master Antenna Television System (MATV) carrying the closed-circuit signal to the Rayburn Building. Videotaping of daily House proceedings was the responsibility of the House Recording Studio.

The three surveillance type cameras used during the test were mounted in stationary positions on the railings in front of the visitors' galleries. One camera, near the middle of the gallery, focused on the Speaker's dais and the lecterns in the well of the House. The other two were located in the southeast and southwest corners of the gallery and were focused on either of the majority or minority committee tables. Both corner cameras were equipped with zoom lenses, but the Speaker's camera had only a 100 mm lens. From the three camera locations and by utilization of the zoom lenses all areas of the House floor were within camera range. The existing House sound system provided the audio portion of the television test. In choosing their various shots, camera operators were allowed no editorial judgment and, in view of the primitive camera arrangement, artistic composition was out of the question.

Several changes occurred in the overall television system as the ninety-day test progressed. Remote controlled pan and tilt mechanisms were added to the cameras and a minisplit effects and character generator was added to the video system. The effects/character generator allowed creation of a split or quarter-screen visual effect whereby two or four different scenes could share the television screen simultaneously. The character generator allowed various information such as speaker identification, bill titles, etc. to be electronically inserted into a scene. The House's electronic voting system that automatically tallied votes on a television viewing screen was modified to feed into the House television system. Since the select committee realized that color cameras were necessary if House telecasts eventually were to be made available to broadcasters, a number of manufacturers were invited to test their cameras under actual House conditions. House lighting, sufficient for the monochrome cameras in use during the test, was also gradually improved for the eventuality of color television. Finally, improvements in the existing MATV relay system were made and plans were completed to extend closed-circuit coverage to the Cannon and Longworth House Office Buildings.[47]

The test evaluation, mandated by the Anderson Resolution, was conducted by the select committee with input from the House Rules Committee. After seventy-five of the test's ninety legislative days, a questionnaire designed to ascertain uses of and attitudes toward House television was distributed to 150 House members. Few respondents indicated any discernible adverse effects of House television on their performance or on House procedure in general. Some said that debate had lengthened, but others said that television's presence had improved debate. Only one respondent said that he felt "personally inconvenienced or inhibited" by the television cameras. Questioned on television's effects on House proceedings in the event telecasts became public, twenty-two respondents expected a positive impact (e.g., improved chamber attendance and better preparation for debate); seventeen expected a negative impact (e.g., "grandstanding" and lengthier sessions); and forty-nine expected a mixture of both positive and negative effects.

Respondents who could receive the closed-circuit telecasts indicated a variety of ways they had used them, including 1) following debate while tending to minor chores such as signing mail, 2) checking the status of debate prior to reaching the House floor, 3) obtaining early voting trends prior to reaching the floor, 4) monitoring of debate by staff personnel in the absence of the House member, and 5) viewing of debate by constituents while waiting in members' offices.

The final section of the questionnaire dealt with the future of House television. Most respondents favored making daily gavel-to-gavel coverage available to the public. A strong preference was also shown for the House retaining control of any future television coverage system. And whereas preference was shown for a system controlled at the Speaker's discretion, an even stronger preference was shown for a system controlled by a House committee.[48]

Upon completion of the ninety-day test, the select committee concluded that the test had successfully demonstrated the "feasibility of broadcast coverage of House proceedings" and that "neither technical nor policy considerations stand in the way of early development of a permanent [House broadcasting] system." On the technical side, the committee concluded that color "minicameras," similar to ones already tested in the House chamber, could be used to televise proceedings "unobtrusively, without the need for significant reconstruction of the Chamber, additional personnel, greatly enhanced or otherwise intrusive lighting, bulky equipment, and in a manner which fully protects the decorum and integrity of the House." Lastly, the committee concluded that the "operation, management, and supervision" of the House television system "should be a responsibility of the House itself and *should not be delegated* or contracted out to groups outside the Congress." (Emphasis added.)

Based on these conclusions, the committee recommended that the Speaker extend the ninety-day test to the end of the current session of Congress in order to assure continued television reception by House members already using the service. The committee also recommended that a resolution be adopted prior to the session's adjournment "authorizing establishment of a permanent system of television and radio coverage of the daily proceedings of the House." Provisions to be included in the resolution would insure that coverage of the "daily legislative business of the House be complete, continuous, and unedited"; that it be available to House members on a closed-circuit basis; that it be available to the public through broadcast stations, networks and services accredited by the House Radio-TV Gallery; that commercial or political use of televised House proceedings be prohibited; and that responsibility for implementing the coverage be vested in the Speaker. Additionally, the committee recommended that the Speaker make arrangements with some entity such as the Library of Congress to record House proceedings and to provide an archive to store the recordings.[49]

Rep. Gillis Long (D-La.) fashioned the select committee's recommendations into H.Res. 821 and introduced it on October 6. The measure was referred to the Rules Committee and subjected to two days of hearings on October 13 and 19.[50] Several broadcasters who testified during the hearings were understandably critical of the resolution's insistence on a House-controlled television system. While arguing their case in essentially philosophical terms, the broadcasters cited at least one practical obstacle that would not affect a network-controlled system but which could cause major complications for a House-controlled system. It seemed that union contracts prevented the television networks from airing more than three minutes per day of programming that originated from a non-union source. Since House camera technicians would not be union members, there likely would never be more than a three-minute segment of House proceedings aired during a given day on any network newscast.[51]

(Though the point was never openly broached during these hearings or during earlier hearings on House television, one must question whether the expense of maintaining a pool coverage system was something that broadcasters sincerely wished to bear. Having made their principled stand for First Amendment access privileges, would broadcasters really have been willing to continue their access advocacy by committing the funds necessary to cover congressional floor activity—activity that heretofore had generated little interest among network news personnel?)

Rules Committee member John Anderson objected to the ambiguity of the two H.Res. 821 provisions allowing, at one point, "complete and unedited" television coverage, while allowing at another point "direction and control" of the coverage system by the Speaker. "This raises the obvious question," said Anderson, "as to whether the Speaker might exercise his absolute direction and control over the system to order it to be shut down at will." And as for the relative ease of access to videotapes of House proceedings, Representative Anderson warned that members of the public would be free to purchase the recordings and use them for political and commercial purposes, although members of Congress could not. On the other hand, a congressman would not be prohibited from purchasing the videotapes, sending them to local broadcasters for airing during their newscasts, and charging the purchase to the congressman's expense account.[52]

Following hearings, the Rules Committee decided on October 25 to amend H.Res. 821 by substituting a "clean" resolution, H.Res. 866. The new resolution was reported to the House the next day.[53] The two resolutions were similar, save for a provision in the new measure requiring the Rules Committee to conduct a study of alternative television system control methods for the benefit of the Speaker. The study, though seemingly superfluous in view of the extensive studies already devoted to the subject, would serve two functions: first, it would fulfill the requirement outlined by the Anderson Resolution (H.Res. 404) for a thorough evaluation of the recently completed ninety-day television test. The select committee's evaluation had fulfilled the requirement to some extent but not to the total satisfaction of the Rules Committee. The second function would be to provide one final and thorough study of possible coverage systems. As Rules Committee member B. F. Sisk explained, "The committee believed that the study was necessary to assure that the Speaker received as much information as possible on all alternatives for broadcasting before he made a decision on which system to choose."[54]

The fact that Speaker O'Neill would exercise final approval of a House television system underscored the questionable need in preparing an additional report on the matter. His rejection of a system controlled by anyone other than the House would become well known far in advance of the February 15, 1978, completion date of the Rules Committee report.[55] If there was significance of any kind to be found in mandating the report, it seemed to be in the unyielding efforts of certain Rules Committee members to persuade the Speaker to accept a network pool coverage system.

House Resolution 866 came before the House on October 27. Debate was brief and non-substantive. The history of the House television effort was recited and the provisions of H.Res. 866 were outlined, but the controversy engendered by the subject in the past was not to be found. The only House member to raise any strong objections to the resolution was Rep. Leo Ryan (D-Calif.). He insisted that the House was on the verge of changing "from a forum to a theater" and urged his colleagues to "resist pressure to change this [chamber] from a place where reasonable men and women may debate to the kind of place which the Roman Senate became."

Ryan's words were not heeded, though, as the House voted an overwhelming 342 to 44 to pass H.Res. 866.[56] In so doing, permission now was granted the Speaker to continue and expand the closed-circuit television system already in operation. The Rules Committee was authorized to commence work on its study due on February 15 of the following year. And most important, the House embarked on a course that guaranteed the public future televised access to House chamber proceedings.

The Rules Committee's Subcommittee on the Rules and Organization of the House, chaired by Rep. Gillis Long, was given the responsibility for conducting the study authorized by H.Res.

866. Two of the subcommittee's eight members were Representatives Sisk and Anderson, the leading advocates of a network pool system. Their combined persuasive skills would be concentrated not only inside but also outside the subcommittee in the coming months as articles by both extolling the virtues of a network pool television system appeared in leading newspapers.

In the *Washington Post*, Representative Anderson warned that a "major First Amendment controversy is shaping up over who should control the cameras" and that Congress would be strapped with a House controlled system not of its own choosing if the system decision were delegated entirely to the Speaker. Anderson insisted that if the entire House were allowed to vote on the matter, "a majority [would] agree that professional broadcasters should do the broadcasting just as the legislators should do the legislating."[57]

Representative Sisk, writing for the *New York Times*, emphasized the credibility problem Congress would face by operating its own television system. "If the broadcasts appear censored or in any way restricted," he warned, "the validity of the coverage will be questioned. Rather than enhancing the House's credibility, broadcasts that are considered self-serving could tarnish its image."[58]

The *New York Times* also entered the fray editorially by suggesting that rather than an either/or solution to the coverage control issue the House should consider a system to meet its needs as well as the needs of broadcasters.[59] The plan, later endorsed by *Broadcasting* magazine, would allow the House to operate its own closed-circuit system but would also allow broadcasters to move their cameras and microphones into the House chamber to cover important debates. The House's closed-circuit system still could be tapped by television networks and stations for short segments to use during daily newscasts.[60]

As a gesture toward accommodating Representative Anderson's insistence on a House vote, Speaker O'Neill stated during a January 22 television interview that members of the House indeed would be given the opportunity to accept or reject whatever system choice he might make.[61] Anderson remained skeptical of how effective a House vote would be if terms under which the vote might occur were decreed by the Speaker. His skepticism was reinforced when it became known that the Speaker had authorized the Architect of the Capitol to purchase new television cameras and equipment soon after the October 22 vote on H.Res. 866. Since he interpreted that transaction as a *de facto* commitment toward implementing a House controlled television system, Representative Anderson claimed that a House vote now simply would be "on reimbursing the Architect for money already spent."[62]

When the House Rules report was issued on February 15, its primary recommendation that the House operate its own television system marked a decisive defeat for the Sisk/Anderson network pool forces. The official rejection of their system occurred on February 8, as the Rules Committee met to consider its subcommittee's system recommendations. Final efforts by both Sisk and Anderson to persuade the committee to reject the House-controlled system in favor of a network pool system failed to win approval. The Rules Committee voted 9 to 6 to accept its subcommittee's recommendations—recommendations that were "obviously more tailored to the Speaker's wishes than the merits of the issue," according to Representative Anderson.[63]

The final draft of the Rules Committee report was presented to Speaker O'Neill on February 15. The body of the report, citing what the committee had described as the most "central, critical, and emotionally charged" question surrounding the matter of House broadcasting, moved directly to an examination of coverage system options. After carefully comparing four of the most frequently mentioned possibilities—a network pool system, a House system, a system managed by the Public Broadcasting Service, and one managed by a new public commission—the committee had concluded that "no single alternative would appear to have a decided advantage over any other" and that "none of the alternatives presents a perfect solution."[64] Clearly, though, the indication was that the committee had directed its major attention only to the House and network pool systems.

Since a choice had to be made between the two, it was requisite that the committee establish the most justifiable bases for whatever recommendation it would make. The committee decided to proceed by looking first at the most serious shortcomings of both coverage systems. For instance, those who opposed the House system alleged that

> House control . . . raises first amendment questions; that it is incompatible with a free society; that it is improper for the House to provide its own news coverage or prevent broadcast journalism from enjoying the same right of focusing its attention on whatever it deems newsworthy as print media journalists enjoy; that both the media and the public will perceive such House coverage as governmentally controlled news and suspect to censorship influences.

On the other hand, those who opposed the network pool system alleged that

> network pool control may produce coverage that is unbalanced, biased, deliberately or accidentally unfair to individual Members, and damaging to the dignity of the House,. . . [and] that broadcast journalism is prone to judge what is newsworthy on the basis of conflict, drama, and humor rather than on the substantive significance of a matter; that television journalists tend to emphasize visual impact over substance because that is the nature of their medium; that when the House is in one of its dull and boring moments the broadcast journalists will not be able to resist searching with their cameras for some visual humor on the floor to maintain viewers' interest and attention.

The Rules Committee responded to both sets of allegations by insisting that a misunderstanding existed in the fundamental purpose for making televised coverage of its floor sessions available to the public. The committee explained that television cameras initially had been allowed into the House chamber as a monitoring aid by which members might stay abreast of floor action while tending to business in their offices. Allowing the public access to this closed-circuit system would not change the system's basic purpose; broadcasters and the public alike simply would be allowed to eavesdrop, as it were, on the monitoring system.

To this, the Rules Committee report added,

> We see no violation of first amendment rights if the House operates the broadcast coverage. On the contrary, the House will not impose

on all broadcast journalists the unchangeable judgment of only one of their colleagues [as would be the case with a single network television director]. Fears of censorship are completely unwarranted. The House has committed itself to providing complete and unedited access to its proceedings, unedited by the House or by any other hand. . . .

It is because of the deeply imbedded news and drama oriented predilection of the broadcast media—perfectly understandable and commendable for their legitimate purpose but inappropriate for what we see as the fundamental purpose of the coverage—that we reject network pool control and recommend House operation of the system.

This general recommendation was accompanied by five specific implementation recommendations. The first was that the coverage system be modeled after the one employed by the Canadian Parliament.[65] Rules Committee staff members had toured the facilities of the Canadian House of Commons television system and had interviewed House Speaker James Jerome in late January 1978 on the effects television had had on Canadian House proceedings.[66] The staff had come from that meeting favorably impressed by what it had learned.

The second recommendation called for the Speaker to delegate management of the television system to either an existing or a new House committee. The committee would be responsible for general system oversight; for review of broadcast policies, quality and costs; for formulating rules to govern the system; for adjudicating complaints about system operations; for planning for recording of House sessions and setting fees for purchase of recordings; and for periodically incorporating technological innovations into the system.

The report's third recommendation cautioned that

The Speaker should authorize broadcasting to begin only after he and the committee he selects, on the basis of tests conducted with the actual equipment and under the actual lighting and camera conditions to be used, are satisfied that the coverage produces an acceptable level of picture, sound, and production quality without undue discomfort, distraction, or inconvenience for Members on the floor of the House. The Speaker should seek, and the House should provide, funds sufficient to obtain expert advice, quality equipment, and professionally competent staff required to achieve and maintain these conditions.

This particular recommendation was based on a number of technical problems in the closed-circuit system that had been used during the ninety-day television test. Videotapes of some of the proceedings showed that House lighting had caused pronounced shadows at the eyes and chins, called "raccoon effects"; moreover, the automatic camera operation had produced "amateurish pictures unworthy of the dignity of the House."[67]

As for the matter of appropriating sufficient funds to construct a first-rate operation, the Rules Committee had learned another valuable lesson from the Canadians. When the committee staff members had interviewed Canadian House Speaker Jerome they had asked about the feeling among House members toward the nearly $5 million construction cost of their television system.[68] Jerome had answered that

> there was never any doubt that the only commitment that was possible was to high quality. I think properly we felt all along that anything that the House of Commons does, should be done in a first class style, and therefore if we are going to television, it ought to be, it must be, a first class operation, and I think that is what we have done. I think the thought would have been that if a first class way of doing it is more than we can afford to do, then let's not do it.[69]

The Rules Committee report next recommended that several legal and administrative arrangements be completed before opening House television to the public. Among these were clarification of the legal standing of recordings in interpreting the intent of the House, statutory prohibition of political use and commercial sponsorship of House telecasts, and amendment of House rules to authorize complete and unedited House broadcasts (except for secret sessions) and to describe the Speaker's authority over the broadcasts.

Although H.Res. 866 already provided for the final two items, the Rules Committee noted that the authority of that resolution would expire with the adjournment of the Ninety-fifth Congress. New rules or statutes would be necessary to reinforce the two provisions.

The final committee recommendation called for a study of the potential for transmitting House telecasts via domestic communications satellites and cable television.[70] Here again, it was ob-

Congress Considers Chamber Television   109

vious that the experience of the Canadian House of Commons with cable and satellite distribution of its telecasts[71] had made a lasting impression on the Rules Committee staff.

The Rules Committee report generated considerable comment from broadcast journalists. Even before the report's release the Coalition for Professional Broadcast Coverage of the House Floor, anticipating what the committee would recommend, issued a statement urging committee members to reject a House-controlled television coverage system. The coalition, whose members included all the national broadcast network news organizations, the two national news wire services, the Society of Professional Journalists, and the National Association of Broadcasters, argued that a House-controlled system would be "distinctly against the public interest" and that "the job of reporting the House [should] be left strictly to the reporter."[72]

Criticism continued as the Radio Television News Directors Association (RTNDA) expressed "regret" at the committee's decision. The association charged that the committee "dismissed much too lightly the two most significant arguments against the House covering itself"—barring free access to reporting by broadcast journalists and loss of public credibility in a coverage system controlled by those being covered.[73] The National News Council (NNC) agreed with the RTNDA's views and issued a statement urging that "the transmittal of congressional proceedings for news purposes be unfettered—free of the taint of any form of government control." The NNC further stated, "Such government control of the means of obtaining news is surely as much of a contravention of First Amendment guarantees of freedom of the press as government control of a newspaper devoted to reporting the happenings of Congress would be."[74]

Speaker O'Neill was undaunted by the barrage of criticism and proceeded with his television implementation plans. By June 8, 1978, he was prepared to announce completion of cabling to the remaining House office buildings, enabling all House members now to receive closed-circuit television feeds from the House chamber. Quite unexpectedly, though, he followed that announcement with a more momentous one:

Under the provisions of [H.Res. 866], all accredited news media will be allowed beginning on Monday, June 12, to plug into the House microphone systems and to distribute full audio coverage of House proceedings for an indefinite trial period.

The Chair desires to stress that none of such broadcasts may be used for any commercial or political purposes. The Chair requests the cooperation of all parties involved in this endeavor to assure that the dignity and integrity of the proceedings of the House are upheld.[75]

The decision to allow live radio coverage was in response to a request from Associated Press (AP) Radio. Speaker O'Neill agreed to the request but only on the condition that no coverage activity take place in the House gallery. The Speaker felt that the potential for disruption to House order would be too great if all news organizations wishing to use the audio service were allowed to report from inside the House chamber.[76]

The commentator covering the first broadcast House session, AP Radio's Charles Van Dyke, was confined to viewing the floor proceedings via a television monitor tapped into the House closed-circuit system. Van Dyke welcomed the radio audience by remarking, "As one who has been listening to the House for a few years,. . . I can predict that you'll find it, at times, interesting, sometimes maddening, occasionally exciting and sometimes plain boring." AP Radio elected to carry only five minutes of live coverage, but that was five minutes more than any other network. NBC, CBS, ABC, NPR, Mutual and UPI Audio carried only taped excerpts during their regular news programs later in the day.[77]

Two days after radio coverage of the House began, an opportunity arose for House members to vote on their preference for a television control system. The occasion came indirectly as the House considered an appropriations bill (H.R. 12935) for legislative expenditures in the coming year.[78] As it happened, a portion of the bill would fund the purchase of television cameras. Rep. John Anderson argued that passage of the bill, allowing as it did for buying the cameras, meant a *de facto* acceptance of the Speaker's favored House-controlled television system. Anderson, who had pressed steadfastly for a House vote on the control system issue (a vote promised by Speaker O'Neill), felt it necessary now to propose an amendment whose language would guarantee that House members' prerogatives in the matter be maintained. The amendment read, "No part of the funds appropriated in this Act shall be used to purchase new color television cameras and related equipment for the purpose of broadcasting the proceedings of the House except by the prior approval of the House and in accordance with the provisions of House Resolution 866."

Rep. Gillis Long went one step further by suggesting that the entire matter could be settled then and there by acting on a second proposed amendment that would allow the House to vote on a preferred television control system. With that, the House voted a close 249 to 133 to kill the Anderson amendment and immediately considered the Long amendment, which read, "No funds in this bill may be used to implement a system for televising and broadcasting the proceedings of the House pursuant to House Resolution 866, 95th Congress, under which the TV cameras in the Chamber are controlled and operated by persons not in the employ of the House."

At this point, Representative Anderson made his final appeal for a network pool television system, asking his colleagues "to reflect very carefully . . . on the nature of the decision that we make, because I think it could have important consequences as to whether or not the American people accept the televised proceedings of this House as really the authentic kind of journalism that ought to attach to televised proceedings."

House Majority Leader Jim Wright (D-Tex.) countered Anderson's plea with one of his own:

The question we are dealing with is not, as the gentleman from Illinois suggests, the integrity of the journalistic profession. The question at issue is the integrity of the House of Representatives.

The matter at issue is not the freedom of the press. The matter at issue is the responsibility of the Congress and whether we shall assert it.

We are not trying to pass judgment . . . on the journalistic skill or objectivity of network journalism. But I think we are called upon to pass a judgment upon our own capacity to manage and control the business of this House with which we are entrusted. The question is whether we have confidence in the U.S. House of Representatives to record its own proceedings with dignity and integrity as an historic record for now and for the future.

If we do not have sufficient confidence in ourselves to do this, then I suggest we have no business holding ourselves out as Representatives of the American public and trustees of the Republic.

The vote was 235 to 150 in favor of the Long amendment.[79] Thus, the House would control its own television coverage system, and Speaker O'Neill would retain full authority for its implementation.

6 · Television Enters the House While the Senate Delays the Inevitable

The U.S. House of Representatives would make history in 1979 as it moved toward implementing televised coverage of its chamber proceedings. The first sign that implementation was under way came when Majority Leader Jim Wright proposed that House rules for the convening Ninety-sixth Congress be amended to include a clause providing for a closed-circuit television system that would enable each House member's office to receive coverage of House floor activity. Control and direction of the system would be under the House Speaker's initial authority, but he could delegate whatever system responsibilities he chose. Although the rules would allow broadcasters access to House telecasts, commercial sponsorship of the telecasts would be prohibited, except when they were part of a regular news or documentary program. Finally, the rules would prohibit House members from using recorded floor proceedings for political purposes.[1]

Rep. John Anderson argued that regardless of the provision prohibiting use of recordings, the proposed rules still would allow House members the privilege of purchasing tapes of floor speeches and sending them to constituents for whatever purposes they might choose. Representative Wright agreed that House members would have that privilege but said it would be comparable to supplying copies of the *Congressional Record* to constituents. Since that practice had not been "regularly abused" by

House members, Wright saw no reason to believe that purchase of recordings would be abused either. Anderson's argument was discounted, and the amended House rules were adopted.[2]

The practice that so concerned Representative Anderson had begun in the previous Congress when House members were allowed to distribute audiotape recordings of their floor remarks to constituents, especially local radio stations. With televised House proceedings beginning in the near future, videotape recordings would soon be as available as audiotapes had been. Anderson did not oppose the purely informational functions served by the recordings; he opposed what he considered to be their potentially abusive political use.[3]

Representative Anderson's views were supported editorially by the *Washington Post*:

> It's not as though members of Congress don't already have ample facilities for making radio and television tapes to ship back home at public expense. But those materials are more clearly self-produced and thus as suspect as any other press release. Cuts from the floor debates will have an institutional ring of objectivity and authenticity that may increase their chances of being used on the evening news. And that compounds the problem, because there will be no assurance that the tapes are really accurate at all. An incumbent could easily edit a tape of a floor speech to eliminate verbal gaffes, much as the Congressional Record is tidied up every day. Beyond that, tapes could be cut and spliced to distort the debate or put opposing viewpoints in an unflattering light.[4]

In an effort to eliminate any possibilities that videotapes might be used abusively, Representative Anderson wrote to Rep. Charlie Rose (D-N.C.), Chairman of the Speaker's Broadcast Advisory Committee, asking that distribution of floor recordings to local broadcasters be prohibited.[5] The Broadcast Advisory Committee, consisting of Rose, Representatives Jack Brooks, Gillis Long and David Stockman (R-Mich.), had been established in late 1978 to assist the Speaker in implementing and managing the House broadcasting system.[6] In his reply to Anderson, Representative Rose said that his committee would consider the matter but for the present withheld making a commitment to any specific action.[7]

Rose later expressed doubt that House members would or could abuse the privilege of purchasing videotapes for political purposes. In the first place, said Rose, the news value of a recording would be diminished considerably by a one-day delay before members could order recorded excerpts. The delay resulted while awaiting publication of the *Congressional Record* in which time cues, appearing periodically throughout the House section, were needed to specify whatever speeches or debates were to be copied. The time cues (e.g., ☐ 1430 as a designation for 2:30 P.M.) were introduced at the beginning of the Ninety-sixth Congress in anticipation of televised House sessions. Beyond the one-day delay, House members also would have to wait their turn as videotape copies were made in the order of their request and only during a House recess.[8]

Operational matters also occupied the attention of the Broadcast Advisory Committee in early 1979. The panel retained a staff of consultants to design the most functional and the best quality television system for the House. The consultants eventually designed a system consisting of six color cameras and accompanying hardware with a purchase price of approximately $1.2 million. Once purchased, the system was installed by House employees. The cameras were attached to railings in front of the visitors and the press galleries. A control room from which the television cameras could be remotely operated was constructed in a basement room of the Capitol. The production technicians necessary to operate the system were hired by the Clerk of the House, who would be responsible for the system's daily operation. Following the lead of the Canadian House of Commons, professional broadcasters with at least five years' experience were hired to fill the twelve production positions. The entire House television system was ready for closed-circuit testing to begin on February 19, 1979.[9]

One month later, on March 19, the House was prepared to open its televised proceedings to the public. Rep. Albert Gore (D-Tenn.) set an optimistic tone for the momentous day as he addressed his colleagues from the House floor: "Television will change this institution . . . just as it has changed the executive branch, but the good will far outweigh the bad. From this day forward every Member of this body must ask himself or herself how many Americans are listening to the debates which are made." Gore went on to predict that as soon as "the House becomes comfortable with the changes brought by television coverage, the news media will be allowed to bring its own cameras into this Chamber."[10]

The first-day television audience witnessed two and one-half hours of House debate on assorted topics including the Strategic Materials Stockpiling Act, a bill to legalize the shipment of lottery materials overseas, and resolutions to create a special committee to study the House committee system and to pay for a recently purchased computer.[11]

The commercial television networks gave scant attention to the inaugural telecast. Whether in deference to the union rule that forbade carrying more than three minutes of the proceedings or in a gesture of resentment over the House-controlled television system, all three networks aired only brief taped excerpts of the day's events in the House. However, PBS elected to carry the House proceedings live and in their entirety. The local Washington PBS station, WETA, originated the coverage from the House television feed.[12] An advertisement heralding WETA's presentation of an "Open House on Capitol Hill" appeared in the entertainment section of the *Washington Post*.[13]

The only viewers able to see full-time, gavel-to-gavel coverage of House sessions throughout the first week of their telecast—and every week thereafter—were those subscribing to a cable television service which was linked to a unique operation known as the Cable Satellite Public Affairs Network or C-SPAN. Although C-SPAN reached some 200 communities during its first week of operation,[14] approximately 170 more were added to its coverage area less than two weeks later.[15] As the third anniversary of televised House proceedings approached in March 1982, C-SPAN was serving nearly 1,200 cable systems in all fifty states, reaching an audience of approximately eleven million cable television households.[16]

RECORDINGS OF HOUSE PROCEEDINGS

One of the benefits of televised House proceedings was supposed to be the record of daily events that videotape recordings would provide. But due to the expense of purchasing and storing the tape, a decision not to retain video recordings was made shortly after the House began recording its floor sessions.[17] Instead, video recordings would be retained for only two months beyond their original recording date before being "recycled" (i.e., erased and used again). Audio recordings would be retained indefinitely in the Library of Congress.[18]

Anyone wishing to purchase a video or audiotape duplicate of House floor proceedings can do so. House members have the advantage of charging the purchases to their office account "if the tapes are to be used in direct support of their official representative duties."[19] The tapes must be ordered through the House Clerk and purchased in either reel-to-reel or cassette formats.[20]

The possibility raised by Rep. John Anderson that House members might abuse the privilege of videotape purchase appeared to diminish as time passed. Members did purchase recordings, but the use they had in mind could be described as only mildly political. As an example, Rep. Pat Williams (D-Mont.) ordered a videotape of opening ceremonies during the first day of televised proceedings for his state's historical society. And Rep. Edward Derwinski (R-Ill.) ordered a videotape of his floor speech on disarmament to make available to high school social studies classes and civic groups in his district.[21]

Events in late 1982, however, changed matters dramatically. A campaign consultant to G. Douglas Stephens, a Democrat challenging the House seat held by Robert Michel (R-Ill.), had recorded some of Michel's remarks from C-SPAN transmitted House proceedings and had used the recordings in one of Stephens's campaign commercials.[22] Ironically, the first person to use House recordings in a partisan, political way turned out not to be a member of the House, as Representative Anderson had thought it would be, but rather a challenger to an incumbent. Brian Lamb, C-SPAN President, said the situation was "inevitable" and noted that Representative Michel, the "victim" as it were, had been an ardent supporter of House television.[23]

Stephens had not technically violated any House rules since rules prohibiting political use of recordings pertain only to House members. Rep. Charlie Rose had introduced a bill (H.R. 5824) in November 1979 that would have extended the prohibition to non-incumbents, but lack of support soon forced Rose to abandon the measure.²⁴ The bill prohibited broadcasters and cable operators from airing recordings of House floor proceedings "for the purpose of influencing the outcome of an election." Broadcasters, who opposed the restrictions the bill would place on them, were supported by Rep. Lionel Van Deerlin (D-Calif.), Chairman of the House Commerce Subcommittee on Communications to whom the Rose bill was referred. Although a hearing for the bill was scheduled in January 1980, it was postponed when no one could be found to testify in the bill's behalf.²⁵

The Stephens taping incident promised to be a political "hot potato." On December 20, Rep. Guy Vander Jagt (R-Mich.), Republican Congressional Committee Chairman, wrote Rep. Tony Coelho (D-Calif.), chairman of the Democratic Congressional Campaign Committee, asking that the Democrats pledge to withhold support from members of their party not abiding by House rules on recordings. Vander Jagt warned that the only alternative to such a pledge would be "unrestrained commercial and political use of House coverage," a prospect that, in Vander Jagt's words, "would be more unpleasant for the Democratic majority than for the Republican minority."²⁶

The matter, unresolved as of this writing, placed C-SPAN in a delicate position, since its service had unwittingly provided the fuel for the controversy. C-SPAN's Brian Lamb could only hope that the incident would not be repeated, but he confessed, "We can't police the use made of the coverage."²⁷

TELEVISION AWAITS SENATE INVITATION

The chances for televised Senate proceedings seemed dependent on the success of House television. Senate Majority Leader Robert Byrd indicated in March 1979 that he would study the progress of the House television experiment before once more attempting to interest the Senate in implementing similar coverage.²⁸ Meanwhile, Senate Minority Leader Howard Baker began a move among his Republican colleagues to allow televised coverage of Senate debate on the Strategic Arms Limitation Treaty (SALT) scheduled for sometime in late 1979.²⁹ A resolution to that effect (S.Res. 253) had been introduced in October,³⁰ but the SALT debate became a moot issue, at least for the Ninety-sixth Congress, when the Soviet Union invaded Afghanistan.

Interest in Senate chamber television was rekindled as the Ninety-seventh Congress convened. On January 6, 1981, Senator Baker, now the Majority Leader, introduced S.Res. 20, a measure that would allow continuous televised coverage of Senate floor proceedings. Live telecasts and recordings would be available to whoever wished to use them, and implementation of the Senate television system would be controlled initially by the Senate Rules Committee.[31]

A C-SPAN survey conducted shortly after introduction of S.Res. 20 indicated a slight majority of the full Senate in favor of television coverage. Fifty-seven senators either strongly favored or leaned toward favoring coverage, while nineteen were firmly opposed. The remainder were either undecided or uncommitted.[32] Though in the minority, those nineteen senators opposing chamber television were led by the formidable Russell Long (D-La.), whose parliamentary strategy would impede progress of the Baker resolution during the coming months.

The Rules Committee began three days of hearings on S.Res. 20 on April 8. Committee Chairman Charles Mathias (R-Md.), a strong proponent of Senate television, opened proceedings with a request that his colleagues "adopt an openminded attitude toward the proposal that is before us." Senator Mathias listed three considerations that were to guide his committee's hearings: 1) the "technical aspects of the issue," i.e., lighting and camera needs in the Senate chamber; 2) the "institutional aspects," i.e., the impact television might have on floor debate; and 3) the matter of cost.[33]

Senator Baker, the first to testify, declared, "There are no insurmountable lighting, temperature, camera location, or editorial control problems [with Senate television]. . . . The most difficult issue . . . is more of a philosophical nature; that is: Can the Senate effectively serve its deliberative role with the people watching our every move?" In answer to his own question, Baker cited "four serious and compelling reasons to believe the Senate will function better with cameras permitted in the Chamber." The first was a return of public confidence in the body. Noting how public opinion polls indicated low esteem for the Senate, Baker suggested that it was "unrealistic to expect public support when we won't let them see us doing what we do in the legislative process." Senator Baker's second reason was to help break through the "cocoon-like atmosphere" of secrecy that so pervades Washington. His third reason was to gain an effective balance with the White House's frequent and easy access to the media. And the senator's final reason was his feeling that television could restore the Senate's lost character as "a great debating group, a great deliberative body, and a great public forum."[34]

Senator Baker's arguments in favor of Senate television were not unlike those heard only a few years earlier in the House. Many of the arguments opposing Senate television likewise mirrored those once heard in the House. There was, for instance, the traditionalists' view from Sen. John Warner (R-Va.) that the Senate had survived very well for more than two centuries without television, so why tinker with the system now? Senator Baker answered that "the genius of the system has been its ability to evolve, to change, to respond to change, to recognize that things must be done in a different way."[35]

The most vehement opposition came from Senator Long. He insisted that "to put the Senate on television will prove to be a very bad mistake." Long agreed that the quality of Senate debate had deteriorated ("The greatest surplus commodity we have in the Congress," said the senator, "are speeches that need never have been made, speeches that fail to improve on silence") but insisted that television would hardly improve its quality. Television would, however, increase the length of speeches, Senator Long felt, as each senator spoke not to his colleagues but to his constituents viewing at home. Long also cited the possibility that presidential aspirants, of whom there are always a few in the Senate, would take advantage of their national forum in the Senate chamber for daily campaign speeches. Given the Senate's rule that allows virtually unlimited debate (unless the unanimous consent rule can be invoked), it would be difficult to restrain a speaker who is determined to talk. Senator Long concluded his remarks by arguing that television would have a chilling effect on the "honest, free exchange of views" typical of Senate debate.[36]

An assessment of television's role in the Senate was the subject of a special study prepared for the Rules Committee by the Congressional Research Service (CRS). One study item seemed of special interest to the senators, particularly to Russell Long: that of television's effect on Senate floor proceedings. Stanley Bach of the CRS agreed that television likely could inspire longer speeches. There might also be an increase in special-order requests whereby senators are allowed to speak on subjects unrelated to legislative business. In particular, Bach saw the possibility that senators might arrange special-order speeches early in the day so that their statements could be recorded by networks in time to use during evening newscasts. The chance that this might happen was enhanced by the House experience with an increase in one-minute speeches delivered at the beginning of each day's proceedings. The timely, well-designed and brief speeches often found their way onto evening network newscasts. Whether this would happen with the Senate was, of course, only conjecture, and in that respect Bach insisted that it was just as likely that "television coverage would encourage Senators to limit the length and frequency of their floor statements."[37]

Turning to hardware requirements, the committee staff reported that a test conducted by television network personnel in early February 1981 indicated that the chamber's light level would have to be raised to accommodate television and that it could be raised sufficiently without causing glare or discomfort to senators.[38] The cost of upgrading the lighting was estimated at nearly $90 thousand.[39] Additional testing by Senate Recording Studio personnel indicated that as many as eight studio cameras mounted on gallery railings would be necessary to cover the Senate. Camera needs of the Senate differed significantly from those of the House in that senators normally speak from individual desks located throughout the Senate chamber, whereas House members speak only from specific rostrum or table locations near the well of the House. Senate television cameras would have to be of sufficient number and placement so as to provide a clear frontal as well as profile shot of each senator from wherever he might be speaking.[40]

George M. White, Architect of the Capitol, testified that a minimum of five cameras would be needed to cover the Senate.

He estimated that a five-camera system plus videotape recorders, control room, other video-related accessories and a new sound system to provide broadcast quality audio would cost just below $3 million. An eight-camera system would cost an estimated $1.3 million more. White also pointed out that wiring necessary for television had already been installed in the Senate chamber.[41]

The Senate would rely on the same cable distribution method that was currently carrying House telecasts. And although the Cable Satellite Public Affairs Network appeared willing to provide the relay service, there was one major hitch: C-SPAN leased only one satellite transponder and could therefore transmit on only one channel. That meant that the House and Senate, which meet at approximately the same hours, could not be carried simultaneously. According to C-SPAN spokesman John Saeman, proceedings in one chamber would have to be carried live while the proceedings in the other would have to be recorded and aired later. Eventually, said Saeman, C-SPAN planned to lease more satellite space, making it possible to air both the Senate and House proceedings live.[42]

The Rules Committee deliberated on S.Res. 20 during summer 1981. Though there appeared no major committee opposition to Senate chamber broadcasting in general, there did emerge one strong advocate for radio coverage exclusively. Sen. Wendell Ford (D-Ky.) complained that the $4.5-$5 million installation expense and $400-$600 thousand annual operating/maintenance cost of a Senate television system were excessive, especially in light of current Senate efforts to reduce government spending.[43] Besides, radio had already proved itself adaptable to the Senate with National Public Radio's broadcast of the Panama Canal Treaty debate.

Senator Ford's arguments were nearly but not entirely compelling as the Rules Committee voted 7 to 5 to defeat his proposed S.Res. 20 amendment which for the present would have provided for radio but not television coverage of the Senate. That was followed by a unanimous vote on July 8, 1981, to report S.Res. 20 to the full Senate. The Rules Committee indicated it stood ready with an implementation procedure by which it would oversee television facility construction, installation and testing by the Architect of the Capitol and personnel recruitment by the

Senate Sergeant of Arms.[44] Notable in the committee's pronouncement was the absence of any indication that an entity other than the Senate itself would control the television system.

In early February 1982, just after the second session of the Ninety-seventh Congress had convened, Sen. Howard Baker introduced a Senate motion to proceed with consideration of S.Res. 20. The senator parenthetically remarked that he had spotted some extra rolls of cough drops in Senator Long's desk drawer—a clear indication that Long might be planning a filibuster to defeat the Baker motion.[45] That was precisely the case, as Senator Long began a defense of his position that would carry through to the following day. Essentially, Long only repeated and reinforced arguments he had made during his earlier Rules Committee appearance. He asserted that senators, most of whom spend no more than ten percent of their time on the Senate floor, would be forced to increase that time if television were present.[46] And, said Long, "when you place an enormous premium on a Senator being here on the floor and making a speech, he is going to do a lot more of it."[47]

Senator Baker disputed the possibility that television automatically meant more individual appearances and longer speeches in the Senate chamber. He noted, for example, that since the arrival of television the House had reduced its chamber sessions from 1,116 hours during the second session of the Ninety-fifth Congress to 653 hours during the first session of the Ninety-sixth Congress.[48] Senator Long would later counter Baker's figures with some of his own showing that although the House indeed had been in session fewer hours during the time in question, there nonetheless were fewer bills considered and more time spent on each bill.[49]

Sen. John Stennis (D-Miss.) joined Russell Long's opposition. Stennis complained that television would prove embarrassing to the Senate by allowing Americans to view what had too frequently become a disorderly assembly of legislators.[50] Arguments like this, suggesting that appearances would reflect badly on the Senate, prompted Sen. Larry Pressler (R-S.Dak.) to say that the chamber's blemishes should be on television. "I think the people have the right to see what is going on in the Senate Chamber. It is supposedly the greatest deliberative body in the world, but if public exposure shows up some failings, perhaps we should change some of our way of doing business."[51]

Opponents of Senate television had managed to take a disproportionate share of time thus far, but Senator Baker finally managed a February 4 roll-call vote on his motion to proceed with consideration of S.Res. 20. The motion was approved by an overwhelming 92 to 3 margin.[52]

The vote was deceiving; while it indicated an endorsement for debating S.Res. 20, it in no way indicated an endorsement of the resolution itself. In fact, by his own count Baker estimated that all but one Senate Democrat and either eight or nine Senate Republicans—a clear majority—opposed the measure.[53] That was hardly the kind of support to inspire optimism, but Baker was determined to push ahead.

Formal floor action on S.Res. 20 began on February 8, 1982.[54] During several hours of debate, there were few new arguments voiced on either side of the Senate television issue. What became obvious to television proponents was the strength of their opposition, especially that of Russell Long, whose continued threat of filibuster made passage of S.Res. 20 a virtual impossibility. Acknowledging the likelihood of his resolution's failure, Senator Baker temporarily withdrew it from consideration only one day after its introduction.[55]

The brief hiatus ended on April 12 as the Senate resumed consideration of S.Res. 20. Debate continued through April 20 when a motion to invoke cloture was brought to a vote. The motion, a procedural tool by which debate is brought to a close, requires that at least two-thirds of the Senate (sixty members) approve it.[56] The motion failed by thirteen votes.[57]

The margin of defeat was a bad omen for S.Res. 20 and served once more to illustrate the strength of Senate television opponents. The typical procedure at this point would be immediate reintroduction of another cloture motion, the idea being that the more often a cloture motion on a specific item comes to vote, the greater the likelihood that a gradually increasing number of senators will vote its approval. Baker followed this procedure but with little optimism for his chances of ending debate. He had the alternative, of course, to move to other matters as he had done in February and then to return to the television debate at some future date, thus allowing more time to gather support. But Senator Long would have none of that. He forced the issue by refusing to allow consideration of any other matters.[58] If debate on S.Res. 20 could not be ended, it would die on the Senate floor without ever having come to a vote.

A breakthrough of sorts occurred on April 21. Senator Baker and Senate Minority Leader Robert Byrd had drawn up an amendment to S.Res. 20 that they hoped would serve as a compromise and would at least keep the measure alive for a while longer. The amendment, if approved, would require that the Rules Committee study the television matter once more, examining especially those areas of concern expressed by opponents of S.Res. 20, and within sixty days from passage of the resolution as amended report recommendations for "such regulations and/or rules changes needed to implement television and/or radio coverage of the Senate."[59]

The compromise worked. Senator Long immediately announced his support for the amendment and even conceded that given the proper circumstances he would not oppose limited Senate television coverage.[60] As he moved for a Senate vote on the amendment, Senator Baker commented, "The most uniformly exercised precedent and the most honored tradition of the Senate is that, one way or the other, we finally arrive at a result, and that is what we have done here." He continued, "Nobody is getting everything he wants. I think it is the best resolution of this issue at this time." The Senate vote was an overwhelming 95 to 1 in favor of the amendment. The amended S.Res. 20 was then passed unanimously by voice vote.[61]

Technically, the vote sent the entire matter back to the Senate Rules Committee which, within the specified sixty-day time limit, would have to report not only recommendations but also a clean resolution embodying implementation procedures and rules for Senate chamber television.

The Rules Committee conducted two additional days of hearings on May 19 and 25 to supplement the information it had previously received during its April and May 1981 hearings. The committee found it impossible to complete its assigned task within sixty days and had to seek two extensions, the first for thirty days and the second for eight days.[62] The extensions were due mainly to the repeated failure for a quorum to gather and to what many believed were delaying maneuvers in the efforts of Sen. Wendell Ford to win support for two S.Res. 20 amendment proposals.[63] He once again introduced an amendment to provide for radio but not television coverage of the Senate chamber. That amendment failed by a clearly partisan 5-to-7 tally. The second Ford amendment called for deferring committee action on S.Res. 20 until after receipt of a report from the Study Group on Senate Practices and Procedures. This special panel had been created by the Senate in April 1982 to study Senate rules and procedures and to recommend alterations that among other things might improve deliberative proceedings in the Senate chamber. Senator Ford argued that the Study Group could provide excellent guidance on rule changes and implementation procedures for television.[64] The second Ford amendment proposal was also defeated by the same 5-to-7 margin as the first.

The 5-to-7 partisan split occurred yet a third time when the Rules Committee voted on July 12 to submit its report to the full Senate. The five minority committee members—Democrats Byrd, Ford, Howard Cannon, Daniel Inouye and Claiborne Pell—attached a dissenting statement to the report. The senators explained that they did not object to Senate television coverage in principle; rather they objected to the cost of implementing the coverage system. "When we are not only struggling to reduce government spending but in the process dangerously reducing many basic social programs affecting millions of Americans," said the Democrats, "to argue that this expenditure for television should be made now approaches legislative irresponsibility." The senators also noted in their dissent the curious action of the Rules Committee's Republican majority: "It is with a mixture of puzzlement and humor that we present these views as 'minority' on the reporting of this resolution when, at the meeting at which it was ordered reported, a majority of the majority favoring its reporting to the Senate expressly reserved the right to vote against it on the Senate floor."[65]

The major committee findings were that no Senate rules would have to be changed to accommodate chamber broadcasts, that voting procedures would remain the same and that television coverage would not alter any parliamentary procedures currently practiced in the Senate chamber.[66] Specific implementation recommendations were incorporated into an original resolution, S.Res. 436, and introduced by Rules Committee Chairman Mathias on July 27, 1982. The measure contained the following provisions:

1) With the exception of closed-door sessions, Senate chamber proceedings would be televised gavel-to-gavel.
2) All television equipment used to provide Senate telecasts would be owned and operated by the Senate.
3) The television system would be constructed under the supervision of the Architect of the Capitol and operated and maintained by the Senate Sergeant at Arms in conjunction with the Senate Recording Studio.
4) A one-time expenditure of $3.5 million would be authorized to cover installation with annual operating expenses funded through normal appropriations.
5) The television cameras would focus only on an individual senator while speaking or on the Senate's presiding officer.
6) The Senate broadcasts would be provided free to qualified recipients.
7) A video and audio recording of Senate proceedings would be produced and made available at cost to authorized persons.
8) Recordings would be permanently stored in the Library of Congress and the National Archives where they would be available to the public for hearing, viewing and/or copying at cost.
9) Persons requesting recordings of Senate proceedings would have to certify that the recordings would not be used for commercial or political purposes.
10) A test period to perfect operational procedures would follow initial equipment installation and television facility construction. Telecasts during this period would not be available for public use. The test would end only after the Senate Majority and Minority Leaders and the chairman and ranking minority member of the Rules Committee were satisfied that telecasts were ready to be seen.[67]

Although it had finally come before the Senate, S.Res. 436 would not be debated until all other business on the current congressional session's agenda was completed, according to a late

July statement from Senator Baker.[68] The delay was indicative of the continued opposition to Senate television, even with the procedural safeguards worked out by the Rules Committee. Senator Long, who earlier had seemed willing to compromise his position, was said near year's end to be "still strongly opposed to televising the Senate" and "prepared for an extended debate" once formal debate on S.Res. 436 began. What is more, a C-SPAN survey released on December 2, 1982, showed only forty senators strongly favoring Senate chamber television. Senator Baker claimed S.Res. 436 had far better support than the C-SPAN survey suggested.[69] Nonetheless, facing Senator Long's threatened filibuster and given the press of higher priority business, Senator Baker decided not to pursue consideration of S.Res. 436 during the remainder of the Ninety-seventh Congress.[70]

The subject of Senate television remained alive, however, as the Ninety-eighth Congress convened in January 1983. In fact, Sen. Peter Domenici (R-N.Mex.) remarked during a television interview program that chances for approving a Senate television resolution continued to improve with the passage of time. And Senator Domenici added, "My gut tells me that it is a very close vote, but he's [Baker] going to work very hard to try on the first three or four months of this year and I think if it's going to happen, it's going to happen then, very early this year."[71]

Something indeed seemed to be in the works when it became known in early February that Senators Baker and Long were about to reach a compromise that would at least allow experimental Senate telecasts, telecasts whose reception would in all likelihood be confined to Senate offices.[72] But the compromise failed,[73] complicated in part by a situation with which the House was now grappling. It so happened that during the previous fall's election one of the House member's non-incumbent opponents had videotaped several of the member's speeches and had used them in a partisan fashion.[74] If this could happen in the House it could happen in the Senate too, so went the argument of Senate television opponents.

That hurdle placed in the way of Senate television did not stop Sen. Charles Mathias from introducing S.Res. 66 on February 16. The new resolution was identical to the now deceased

S. Res. 436. Senator Mathias accompanied his introduction with these comments:

> As we all know, innovation does not come quickly to the Congress, especially to this body. We need not worry that we are rushing into this matter with undue haste. The idea has been with us in one form or another since the mid–1940's. . . . Surely we cannot be accused of the type of haste that makes waste.
>
> As we all know, too, innovation does not come to this body without a great deal of consideration. The proposal to broadcast Senate floor proceedings has been studied and restudied by the Senate itself and others.
>
> But even the most exhaustive studies must come to an end. We have studied enough. Again, I say, its time has come.[75]

Senate Resolution 66 was sent to the Rules Committee where Chairman Mathias promised quick action.[76] But quick action was not to be, and as this book went to press, the Senate chamber was still without television.

7 · The Impact of Congressional Television

This chapter examines television's effects on congressional committee hearings and chamber proceedings. It also examines effects on participants in and viewers of these activities.

TELEVISION AND CONGRESSIONAL HEARINGS

Much of the literature dealing with the effects of televised congressional hearings comes from the period surrounding the Kefauver and McCarthy Committee hearings of the mid–1950s. Chapter 3 discussed many of the legal issues stemming from these hearings, and as a later chapter documented, some of the issues were not resolved by the time television began its marathon coverage of the Senate Watergate hearings in the early 1970s.

Although information presented thus far has concentrated on the effects of televised hearings on witnesses, there have been profound effects on committee members as well. One recent study, for instance, found that U.S. Senators are sometimes influenced in their choice of committee assignments by the television coverage particular committees receive. Newly elected senators or senators with little tenure in office are said to be more assertive committee interrogators than in the past because of the television coverage their comments might attract.[1]

Members of the Ervin Committee especially were affected by the public attention heaped upon them both during and after their committee's hearings. Letters and phone calls of all kinds flowed into the senators' offices from persons who, among other things, offered gifts, offered to arrange speaking engagements and even proposed marriage to one bachelor committee member.[2] Their moment in the television spotlight had thrust the Ervin Committee members into a celebrity status.

It is one of history's ironies that committee chairman Sam Ervin, who had cared so little for television in the past that he had shunned it during his numerous political campaigns, would become a national symbol of the Watergate hearings. One theory as to why this happened came from David Halberstam:

Ervin became the perfect counterpart to the Nixon White House. He was so artfully unartful, so clearly a man from an era now past, that he gained an extra legitimacy. He was not sleek and pretty. He was what he was, that which he had always been. Television was incidental. Television had found him, he had not found television.[3]

Effects on Viewers

Studies of the effects of televised congressional hearings on viewers have concluded that any such observable effects are attitudinal in nature; only rarely have hearings stimulated viewers to actively involve themselves in matters associated directly with the hearings. Even the degree of attitudinal change is marginal, as observed by sociologists Kurt and Gladys Engel Lang: "Opinions change—but seldom that quickly or profoundly. Television is powerful—but coverage of any one event rarely produces sweeping transformations."[4] (As will be noted later, the one exception to this general observation occurred during the Watergate hearings.) When active involvement has been apparent its most frequent manifestations have been letters or phone calls to congressmen or appearances at the voting booth to record either support for or opposition to persons or issues which were the object of a hearing inquiry.

Regardless of how a viewer reacts to what he sees, a televised congressional hearing provides him with a basic source of information. A viewer's interest presumably has been aroused sufficiently beforehand to cause him to seek the information. Moreover, hearing procedures are not so complex as to impede a viewer's comprehension of what is happening or why it is happening, so he should be able to glean as much as he wishes about the hearing's subject matter, depending on how much he can see or how much he chooses to see.

Quite apart from the information-seeking viewer is the one who watches a congressional hearing for the sheer spectacle of it. One ordinarily does not think of hearings as television entertainment, but, nonetheless, those hearings such as the Kefauver, McCarthy and Ervin Committee hearings that have received extended coverage possessed the same viewer appeals as some entertainment programs. One observer referred to the Watergate hearings in particular as containing "in profusion the panoply and ingredients of television courtroom dramas."[5]

The Senate Watergate hearings have become the supreme instrument by which viewer effects of televised congressional hearings are measured. Not surprisingly, researchers were better prepared to study the Watergate hearings than they were earlier hearings. But research of an earlier vintage still has yielded some important data.

A study of the Army-McCarthy hearings' effects on television viewers was conducted by G. D. Wiebe in 1954. Wiebe was interested in whether viewers would be aroused to a "ringing reaffirmation of traditional liberties, and, correspondingly, to a mass rejection of Senator McCarthy for having encroached upon those freedoms." But rather than talk about values such as freedom of speech, freedom to be tried fairly, etc., viewers were more interested in either praising or criticizing hearing participants for such attributes as sticking to their convictions. Wiebe found very little change of attitude among those persons who either supported or opposed McCarthy. Convictions were strengthened, not weakened.

Wiebe also studied the viewer impact of the televised Kefauver Committee hearings. Although he found viewers outraged by committee revelations, their outrage did not arouse any particular action.[6] Once the hearings had ended and once discussion of them had subsided, citizens seemed content to forget about efforts to eradicate any threat posed by organized crime.

The effects of the Senate Watergate hearings on their television audience differed markedly from the above. In terms of audience size alone the Watergate hearings clearly outdid their two mass audience predecessors.[7] And in terms of significant attitudinal change the Watergate hearings audience easily was set apart from the Kefauver and McCarthy audiences.

If the Watergate hearings audience is to be compared with audiences of earlier televised hearings it should be noted that three major points set the former apart from the others. First, more television receivers and thus more television households were present in the 1970s than in the earlier decades. Second, the Watergate hearings focused not so much upon impersonal, abstract events as they did upon the highly visible and personal Presidency. Third, research has shown that as our country has become more reliant upon the mass media for information pertaining to public matters, media users have been conditioned to judge the importance of an issue from the emphasis placed on it by the media. Labeled the media's "agenda-setting function," the principle was shown empirically to have been responsible for so directing public attention to Watergate-related events in correlation with the massive media attention given those events.[8]

Two additional points set the Watergate hearings apart from other televised hearings. One is the extent to which viewers were aware of Watergate events and personalities prior to the telecast of the hearings. As reported by Lang and Lang:

By mid-May [1973], almost everyone knew about Watergate and a majority was now taking it quite seriously—that is viewing it as more than "just politics." A Gallup poll taken between May 11 and 14 said the 96 per cent who had read or heard about Watergate represented "one of the alltime high awareness scores recorded for a major news development."[9]

The second point relates to the number of variables other than television viewing that affected viewer attitudes toward Watergate. In the same way individuals were learning about Watergate events prior to the Watergate hearings, so were they developing attitudes toward those events. The televised hearings were more or less latecomers to the mix of information sources already available. The fact that television rarely acts alone in effecting attitude change was underscored by Joseph T. Klapper in a 1960 study. Klapper coined the term "phenomenistic" for what he regarded as a concept in which particular audience effects result from media influences working amid other nonmedia influences.[10]

As far as direct effects of the televised hearings on viewers, Lang and Lang concluded that attitudes definitely changed as the hearings progressed. Particularly observable were those changes that signaled an accelerated decline in President Nixon's popularity. Other studies recorded much the same results but were more determined to isolate specific beliefs about the Watergate matter and to gauge how these beliefs were affected. One of the major beliefs to be affected related to the magnitude of the problem. Viewers were amazed at the number of illegal acts allegedly perpetrated by members of the Nixon White House. Continued revelations of illegalities meant continued attitudinal adjustment in what one researcher concluded was a gradual "process of education."[11]

A number of studies were conducted to ascertain the impact of the Watergate hearings on the young. Researchers were concerned primarily with how Watergate would affect the "political socialization" process among this country's youth. Obviously, more variables had to be accounted for in this group's source of information and its perception and interpretation of the situation than in an adult group, but the measurement of attitudinal change among children and adolescents exposed to Watergate information was profound. One study showed Watergate to have had a severe effect on grade school children's perception of the presidency. A comparison of 1962 and 1974 measurements of such rating categories as presidential "popularity" and "reliability" showed an overwhelming decline in both categories from one year to the other. Generally, faith and respect in all areas of government fell victim to Watergate.[12] Televised coverage of the Watergate hearings can be surmised to have played a significant role in stimulating youth to adjust their attitudes about this nation's political affairs.

TELEVISION AND CONGRESSIONAL FLOOR SESSIONS

Effects on the House

A number of persons have commented on the possible effects television might have on deliberative congressional floor proceedings. Only recently has it been possible to observe whether predicted effects would be realized in the House. And, of course, there is no indication that as the novelty of television wears away those effects that presently are observable will be of long-term duration.

Several theories have been proposed about the general effects that television has had and might have on Congress. Michael J. Robinson, for instance, has developed two principles which he terms the "First Law" and "Second Law of Videopolitics" to explain television's effects on Congress. Robinson's "First Law" states that "television alters the behavior of institutions in direct proportion to the amount of coverage provided or allowed; the greater the coverage, the more conspicuous the changes." Since Congress has so limited television's coverage of its activity, the institutional changes that have come about in that body have been minimal. Conspicuous change has occurred in the individual behavior of certain institutional members, particularly in the Senate.[13] It will be recalled from Chapter 1 how senators moved far ahead of their House colleagues prior to implementation of House chamber television in accommodating the television medium. As the Senate adapted more of its activities to television, television turned more of its attention to the Senate.

Robinson's "Second Law of Videopolitics" states that "television alters the popularly perceived importance of institutions and individuals in direct proportion to the amount of coverage provided—the greater the coverage, the more important the institution and its members appear to be."[14] This "Second Law" explains several congressional role changes that have occurred since the advent of television. The first of these is the change in status between the House and Senate. As explained in Chapter 1, television's concentration on the Senate and its members has added prestige to that body that thus far has eluded the House.

The lopsided attention the Senate has enjoyed may be eroding, however, due to House chamber television. Sen. Howard Baker has used that possibility to argue his case for Senate television. Responding to an interviewer's question of whether he [Baker] felt the House had gained greater public visibility with its telecasts, the Senator said, "Yes, I do. And I don't begrudge the House that recognition or the public attention they gain. . . . But it does mean that if we don't get television in the Senate in a decade or less, the House will be the dominant partner in the Congressional branch."[15]

A Congressional Research Service report prepared prior to implementation of the House television system discussed how the House might be affected by televised floor proceedings. In some instances the report's hypothetical effects already have been realized, though not necessarily in the manner expected.

The CRS suggested first that television "might cause delays in the transaction of legislative business, requiring possibly the reconsideration or modification of certain legislative procedures." The concern here pertained to the traditional restrictions placed on House debate and the willingness of non-traditionalists to accommodate House members who might want to speak on an issue but who would not ordinarily be given the chance or who would not be given as much time as desired. The demand that more time be given a member to speak could become forceful enough to require that speaking restrictions actually be modified, thus possibly prolonging the time needed to conduct House business. Procedural changes of this kind or of any other kind involving floor activity need not be regarded negatively, though, since such changes could just as easily improve the conduct of this activity.

A second suggested effect was that "many [representatives] likely would become more oriented to television than they are presently, and many might attempt to speak on the floor more frequently." This argument almost predates television itself. The possibility for "grandstanding" always will be present, but studies of state legislatures suggest that television's presence usually has improved the conduct of legislators and improved the quality of debate, and only for short periods following its initial use has television encouraged more than the average amount of speeches.[16] Besides, those House members who would "grandstand" might find their actions to be more deleterious than helpful to their livelihood. As one observer said,

> Given the sort of searching exposure that television could provide, the voters would have a much sounder basis for discerning judgment in filling . . . House seats than they do now. And anyone who contends that the voters are not capable of distinguishing between a ham actor and a solid citizen is not questioning the utility of television but denying one of the premises of the entire democratic system.[17]

Regarding observed effects, prolonged debate on certain issues, particularly the fiscal 1980 budget, has been attributed to House television. As the budget debate moved at half its expected pace in May 1979, Speaker "Tip" O'Neill claimed that more than the usual number of amendments to the budget resolution were being offered by House members eager to get themselves on television. O'Neill was quoted at one point as telling his colleagues that he had "made a terrible mistake" in allowing House telecasts.[18]

The Speaker continued his criticism a few weeks later. This time, prompted by the number of House members who were "taking to the floor to praise people in their districts by name, compliment trusted staff members and give speeches on purely local issues," O'Neill called the effects television had had on the House a "disaster." He noted that by the first week of August 1979 the *Congressional Record* contained 7,000 pages in transcripts of House floor proceedings—a 25 percent increase in pages over the same period during the previous year. The increase was attributed to lengthy television-inspired speeches. Furthermore, at a publication cost of $380 per *Congressional Record* page, Speaker O'Neill held television directly responsible for causing a waste of tax dollars. His solution to the problem was to order a study of the possibility of daily terminating House television coverage at the conclusion of regular legislative business, just before House members begin speaking on nonlegislative matters.[19] But in early September the Speaker dropped plans for his study, saying, "It's pretty clear that the will of the membership is to go along with [gavel-to-gavel coverage]."[20]

A situation such as the Speaker's attempt to short-circuit House television and what might have resulted had he succeeded were anticipated by the CRS report:

> Any possibility under a House resolution or rule that less than complete gavel-to-gavel coverage of House proceedings would be required might influence the House on some future occasions to prevent television coverage of some matter. Such decisions, if not carefully provided for in House rules or guidelines, could embroil the House in controversy.[21]

A fourth effect suggested by the CRS has yet to be realized, although it remains a possibility. As stated, "Party and institutional leaders in the House, as well as other especially articulate or telegenic Members, might be encouraged by fellow Members to assume highly visible roles on the House floor, to focus public attention on issues and party positions."[22]

The CRS next suggested that the House chamber "by becoming more visible to the public might become more important as a place for debate and for influencing Member and public opinion on legislative issues."[23] Implicit in this is the possibility that significant debate on major issues might shift from House committees to the House floor. Not only would House members stand to be persuaded directly by floor speeches, but television viewers also might be persuaded and might be moved to transmit their feelings about issues to their representatives.[24] One congressman has already reported that a constituent, after viewing debate on a particular matter, was moved to call him with a suggestion on how he should vote.[25]

The possibility that House members "likely would revise their remarks in the *Congressional Record* less frequently while the format of the *Record* would likely undergo some changes" was another effect suggested by the CRS report.[26] Thus far, there has been nothing to indicate a dramatic decrease in revision of remarks prior to *Congressional Record* publication. And while its format has undergone some cosmetic changes—"bullets" to indicate material not spoken on the House floor and "cueing" indicators as described in Chapter 6—failure to deal with the revision problem has not enhanced the *Record's* reputation for its sometimes more imaginative than accurate accounts of House debate.

Although revision of speech transcripts destined for the *Congressional Record* has become common practice, an example of how a video or audiotape record of floor activity might affect the practice was provided during the May 1979 House budget debate. At that time a disagreement arose over what two representatives claimed was a discrepancy between the actual statement of a third House member and the revised version of the statement as it appeared in the *Congressional Record*. The two were able to support their claim by purchasing an audiotape containing the actual words of the statement in question.[27]

The final effect predicted by the CRS related to partisan problems that might occur if House members became active distributors of their floor speech recordings.[28] Though chances of this happening remain, they would appear diminished by the cost and distribution delay in acquiring the recordings.

This is not to say that House television could not be used in other "creative" ways to achieve partisan objectives. In fact, its potential in this respect has already been exploited. The House has two unique vehicles for partisan floor speeches that are especially directed to television viewers. One is the "morning hour" where "one-minute speeches," as they are called, are delivered by House members speaking on their choice of subjects.[29] Whereas one-minute speeches are scheduled prior to convening the House for regular daily business, a "special order" period is reserved following the close of House business for individual speeches of longer duration (up to an hour) on any subject.[30] A comparison of figures from 1977 (two years before House television began) with figures from 1981 (two years after House television) showed that the number of one-minute speeches had tripled during the period.[31]

Shortly after television had entered the House chamber, Democrats found themselves on the receiving end of a daily barrage of Republican verbal jabs during the morning hour and special order periods. One House Democrat, in reference to the practice, complained that the periods were being used "to bludgeon us to death each day on nationwide TV."[32] The bludgeoning was especially painful considering that not only were viewers of House proceedings exposed to the speeches, but television networks could also record them, particularly the short morning hour speeches, for airing during evening newscasts.

What House Democrats saw as an abuse of the morning hour came to a head in July 1980 when House Majority Leader Jim Wright, at the urging of his fellow Democrats, announced that hereafter the one-minute speeches would be delivered only at the end of the day. Wright defended his action as necessary for the House to complete its official legislative business. The action and its defense were entirely unacceptable to Republicans who charged that the Majority Leader had "gagged" them. After several days of verbal wrangling over the matter, Representative Wright reversed himself and allowed the morning hour speeches to resume.[33]

It may have been just as well that Wright acquiesced to Republican demands, for Democrats were soon to find the morning hour speeches a convenient way of chiding Republican President Ronald Reagan. This seemed to meet with the full approval of House Speaker O'Neill. In fact, as the third anniversary of House television approached, the Speaker appeared quite pleased generally with the medium's effects in the House. He noted, for instance, that about the only lasting effect television seemed to have had on House proceedings was that the male House members often appeared "in blue shirts, red ties and 'stickem' on their hair."[34]

More scientific data have been added to Speaker O'Neill's decidedly unscientific assessment in attempts to judge television's impact on House proceedings and House members. Two studies in particular, both conducted in 1980, were so directed. In the first, Robinson found positive responses outnumbering the negative by two-to-one after asking House members to record their feelings about House television. And as might be expected, younger members (class of 1978) were much more enthusiastic about television than were their older colleagues (class of 1958).[35]

A survey conducted by staff members of the House Administration Committee reported findings similar to Robinson's. In specific terms, the survey found that House members perceived television as having had a greater effect on their colleagues than on themselves. Sixty-eight percent of those surveyed felt that television's presence had had no influence on their floor attendance, but 17 percent felt that other House members were spending more time on the floor. Questioned about floor debate, 20 percent said that debate was less substantive, whereas 15 percent said it was more substantive. Some 75 percent said that television had not altered their method of preparing floor remarks. Eighty-eight percent said that television's presence had not induced them to make floor speeches that otherwise would not have been made, but 77 percent said their colleagues had increased their speechmaking. Fifty-six percent of the survey respondents said they felt better informed on issues after listening to floor speeches on their office television sets. And a surprising 25 percent said they had increased their familiarity of floor procedure by observing television debate.[36] These last two findings strongly suggest that, owing to television, members of the House are becoming better prepared to perform their official duties.

Effects on the Viewing Audience

This book's first paragraph referred to television as the prime communications medium by which citizens are informed of their government's activity. Though the informational capacity of television is indeed unsurpassed, just how well individuals who view congressional telecasts have been or will be informed or educated or persuaded or otherwise enlightened is mostly speculative at present. Taken in this context the purpose of the remainder of this chapter is to explore some possible effects congressional television, particularly House telecasts, has had and might have on viewers. Before proceeding, some determination must be made of who *can* watch and who *will* watch the telecasts.

The common link among practically all television viewers of House sessions presently is subscription to a cable television service that carries the telecasts. Television network newscasts have carried brief recorded segments of floor debate on a very selective basis, but the only gavel-to-gavel coverage now available is via cable television. Current figures show nearly 27 million households (33 percent of all U.S. television households) subscribing to a cable television service in early 1983.[37] Allowing for a three-per-household measurement, the cable audience amounted to about 81 million individuals. Some 10 million of the 27 million cable households were capable of receiving the C-SPAN service, and according to a January 1982 survey, nearly 9 percent of those households with access to C-SPAN tuned to its programming regularly.[38] Roughly, then, C-SPAN had an audience in 1983 that possibly exceeded 2.5 million individuals.

The key to future House and/or Senate viewership potential rests both in the growth of cable television and in the number of cable systems agreeing to carry the C-SPAN service. Early 1983 estimates showed the prospects for continued cable growth to be very healthy. By 1990, for example, the projected cable television subscribership should be nearly 60 million households.[39] These same projections do not necessarily apply to C-SPAN growth, however. The service fell on hard times in early 1982 and stood to lose nearly half its affiliate cable systems. C-SPAN President Brian Lamb said reasons given for possibly dropping the service ranged from its expense to the minimal viewership attracted by C-SPAN programming.[40]

The next step in determining who can watch C-SPAN telecasts requires a brief demographic analysis of the typical cable television subscriber. Current data show that households in at least three-fourths of this country's 435 congressional districts can tune in to C-SPAN's cable service.[41] And since matters of economics prohibit wiring rural areas for cable, it might be assumed that most cable television subscribers live in urban areas. The additional expense of a subscription fee probably means that most cable subscribers are at least moderately affluent.

Regardless of what other inferences may be drawn in describing cable viewers, one simple factor considerably narrows the House viewer category: Viewers' free hours must correspond with those hours when business is conducted on the House floor. Those hours usually extend from 10 A.M. (the most common time for the House to convene) to 3 or 4 P.M., though some sessions have lasted until late in the evening. Not only do these hours mean that regular viewing requires an individual to station himself before his television set during late morning and early afternoon hours, it also means that his schedule must be flexible enough to match the House's sometimes erratic schedule. Also, since the House meets daily, unless in recess, and usually not on Saturday or Sunday, devoted viewers of House telecasts must set aside those five days on a regular basis.

From these data the emergent audience profile of those able to view House telecasts would seem to include the following: housewives, pre-schoolers, retirees of both sexes, persons of both sexes currently unemployed, and persons who work at night and are home during the day. Of course, the possibility exists for persons falling outside of these categories to record daily House sessions on a home videotape recorder for viewing during evening hours. This hardly could be construed as a common or widespread practice, however.

The growing number of school systems now capable of receiving House telecasts (estimated at over a thousand in 1980)[42] presents some interesting problems. One in particular is that of scheduling class viewing at times when the House is in session. With the House's uncertain schedule, there would be little possibility of pre-arranging viewing sessions at specific times. Classes meeting before 10 A.M. would stand little chance of ever viewing House telecasts. Furthermore, since the weekly agenda of House business is never released until the end of the previous week, and since items on the agenda may be re-scheduled with little prior notice,[43] it would be difficult for instructors to plan class viewing with the anticipation of seeing debate on a particular issue. Of course, class viewing need not be of "live" House sessions. Facilities to record House sessions would eliminate most of the above problems. A system by which a technician might monitor and record daily floor sessions or parts of sessions would facilitate greater utilization of House telecasts for educational purposes.

Assuming a moderate interest among high school teachers in committing class time to viewing House proceedings, it would be difficult to gauge the interest of students (i.e., "captive" viewers) in what they might see. Moreover, it is quite possible that given the choice, the students would prefer not to view the proceedings at all. In fact, the question of just who does (or will) view House telecasts is an intriguing one but not one that is easily answered.

Research has shown that television viewing is normally at its lowest point during those hours when the House is in session. Households using television between 10 A.M. and 4 P.M., Monday through Friday, range between 21 and 27 percent of the total television households in this country. Furthermore, the 10 A.M.–4 P.M. viewing audience normally consists of about 18 percent adult male, 62 percent adult female, 6 percent teenagers and 14 percent children.[44] These numbers provide information only on those persons viewing television, not on what they are viewing. It would not be difficult to deduce what kinds of programs are being watched, since the standard fare of daytime television has consistently been game shows, soap operas and old movies.

Since public affairs programming of any kind has been so alien to daytime television, it is difficult to judge whether the potential audience now attuned to the above program forms has been or could be attracted to viewing House telecasts. And little research seems to exist on which to base any certainties as to who those viewers, if attracted to House telecasts, might be. One study does offer some possibilities for extrapolating the viewer characteristics of one common public affairs programming type to those characteristics that might be expected of House television viewers.

Mark R. Levy studied viewership of the three network news interview programs, "Face the Nation," "Meet the Press," and "Issues and Answers" during October and November 1975. As expected for programs of this type, aired every Sunday during the late morning or early afternoon hours, viewership was low. Only about 6 percent of potential viewers actually watched any of the programs on a regular basis. Further examination of survey data showed that the most common age group for those in the viewer category was fifty-five years and older. Since Levy concluded that viewers of news interview programs "can not be statistically distinguished from non-viewers by either their interest in politics, their level of public affairs knowledge, or their exposure to television and radio news or newspapers," the age characteristic of viewers becomes highly significant. Significant too are the major reasons given for viewing these public affairs programs: "Interview programs give me food for thought"; "I learn new things about public issues from interview programs"; "By watching, I can compare my own ideas with those of the people in the news."[45]

Several reasons exist for assuming that some of the same characteristics of news interview program viewers match those of House television viewers. In the first place, the reasons given for viewing the interview programs show an active, purposive interest among viewers in the program content. The same stimulant would have to draw viewers to House telecasts. Also, viewers who make an effort to watch the interview programs presumably would make the same effort to view House proceedings that occur roughly within the same weekday late morning-early afternoon time frame as the Sunday interview programs. Third, the retirees in the predominantly fifty-five years and older age group of news interview viewers correspond with one of the groups suggested earlier as being best able to view House telecasts.

That age plays a significant role in determining who can and does view televised House proceedings is supported by the political attitudes and predispositions most common among older citizens in this country. As stated by Levy,

> It has been shown that political participation in general increases with age. For some older viewers, then, watching television news interviews is a manifestation of their greater political interest and activity. For other, older respondents (the housebound infirm, for example) exposure may represent a more "passive" behavior. These older people may use interview programs much as they use other television fare, namely as a functional alternative supplying substitute companionship or psychological ties to a world in which they have a decreasing role to play.[46]

Political participation is certainly a factor that should be considered as a predictor of those who might view House telecasts. Political participation as it will be used here excludes confining one's political activity only to voting. Persons who are actively involved in politics between elections have been given many names,[47] but perhaps the most descriptive is that of "Attentive Public" assigned by James N. Rosenau. The Attentive Public consists of those "who communicate, with some regularity, ideas about public affairs to persons with whom they are closely associated (but not to persons whom they do not know)."[48] Four major characteristics distinguish members of the Attentive Public from other citizens: first, they are more often men than women (though this is slowly changing);[49] second, they are more highly educated (in fact, as a person's education increases so does his political participation);[50] third, they are wealthier;[51] and fourth, they more often are employed as professionals or managers than as laborers.[52] Sidney Verba and Norman H. Nie have explained that a close relationship exists between a person occupying a high socio-economic status and his political participation because such an individual "has a greater stake in politics, he has greater skills, more resources, greater awareness of political matter, he is exposed to more communications about politics [and] he interacts with others who participate."[53]

Although Rosenau's Attentive Public conceivably would consist of persons highly interested in viewing televised House proceedings, their availability as potential viewers would have to be suspect. Their interest in political affairs suggests an activism that would hardly allow them time to follow House proceedings on television. Furthermore, their occupational and economic status suggests that members of the Attentive Public would be too busy during the time scheduled for House sessions to allow them time to view the proceedings.

Even if every member of the Attentive Public gave full attention to viewing televised House proceedings, the audience size would be far from overwhelming. One estimate places the Attentive Public at less than 15 percent of the adult population.[54]

What emerges from the foregoing examination is a hypothetical picture of who the viewers of televised House proceedings might most likely be. From what evidence there is, it might be safe to suggest that the regular viewer is either a retired or disabled male or female who once was an active member of the Attentive Public but who now must rely on television viewing as a more convenient way to remain politically informed and involved. Younger members of the Attentive Public probably view House proceedings occasionally and may even attempt to follow debate on a particular issue for an extended period, but time constraints likely would require that viewing be scheduled in advance, according to whatever information might become available on speakers and issues to be covered on a given day. And, of course, students who are required to view televised House proceedings also would fall into the occasional viewer group.

Having ascertained who can and who might view televised House proceedings, attention turns to what a person stands to gain by viewing the proceedings. Obviously, two major objectives of the House in televising its sessions are to show the public what its members do and to inform them as to why they do it. A lesser objective is that of educating the public as to how the House functions. Informing and educating the public in the above are vitally important, since research shows a positive correlation exists between knowledge of Congress and its procedures and public support for the institution.[55]

According to congressional observers and participants, the prospects for informing and educating the public are rather discouraging. Those who have had close associations with congressional proceedings seldom have spoken in complimentary terms of what transpires on the floor of either house. Certainly, the textbook description of floor activity hardly matches the more realistic scene that greets the Senate or House gallery visitor, as described by a former Washington news correspondent:

For the casual onlooker who visits the Capitol in Washington, perspective often depends on which portion of the anatomy he happens to observe. He may watch the main show for hours on end without benefit while its principal activity consists of scattered clusters of men and women sustaining one another in barely audible monotones amidst the vast emptiness of the Senate or House chamber. . . .

The Observer who spends much time on Capitol Hill knows that the chamber drama is at best only a shadow image of what goes on. He counts himself lucky to be present during those celebrated moments when an impassioned oration may markedly affect the course of the legislative process, or, more frequently, when a maladroit argument loses vital votes. But these are the rare spectacles. Most of the time the real drama is going on elsewhere—in the cloakrooms and corridors, in the inner sanctums of the leaders, in the member's own office.[56]

This view of congressional floor proceedings, appearing as it does to be somewhat skeptical of their value, is no more so than the views of many congressmen regarding the same subject. In the words of one former House member,

> Many visitors to the Floor of the House come away disappointed. This is nothing new. . . .
> It is a commonplace that the work of Congress is done in committee. Here the evidence is heard, and the general approach laid down. Changes and amendments can be made on the Floor, but, generally speaking, the action there is confined to crystallizing and distilling the committee process. Debate on crucial issues is the distillate of thousands upon thousands of hours of talk that has preceded. These debates can be well attended and very lively. Or they can be deadly and irrelevant.[57]

It should be realized that the preceding descriptions of floor activity speak of those things that might be visible to a person sitting in the congressional galleries, not to persons viewing the proceedings on television. Since House rules prohibit television cameras from roaming the House chamber, information that could be gleaned by observing House members in their seating areas (e.g., number of members present, identification of those present, conferences among members, reactions to speeches or other chamber events, etc.) is withheld from viewers. The focus of House chamber activity for the television viewer, then, is confined to the major speaking areas just to the front of the Speaker. Thus confined, the television viewer's information about House business is far more aural than visual.

Regardless of whether information is received visually or aurally, the television viewer will have a misconception of what happens on the House floor unless he can place the activity into its proper legislative perspective. Floor debate and passage of a bill or resolution are only two of several major steps that occur between the time legislative measures are conceived and when they are considered by the full House. While these measures "churn through the legislative mill," much preliminary information related to them appears in such published sources as hearing transcripts, the *Congressional Record*, and various executive department documents. Once the measures reach the House floor, only a condensed assortment of arguments are voiced by either side during the ensuing debate. Though the arguments may be substantive enough to sway the viewer (one objective House television was meant to achieve), they likely would not have similar impact on House members.

The fact is that House debate is as much constituent-oriented as colleague-oriented[58] and, therefore, has limited value in the legislative process. Only a few matters that come before the House are even scheduled for debate. According to one source, about one-tenth of the legislative business during a typical Congress is considered controversial enough to be debated for more than thirty minutes.[59] This means that House television viewers are likely to hear very little on any issue (major or otherwise) confronting the House.

Additionally, viewers will have few opportunities to see their local district's representative formally address particular issues during House debate. The size of the 435-member body is a limiting factor in the number of formal speeches any single member can make.[60] Another factor is the House rule for conducting debates. Typically, the only representatives allowed to debate a measure on the House floor are those committee members responsible for reporting the measure under consideration. Even then, the measure's majority and minority managers "dole" out debate time (sometimes no more than two or three minutes per person) to committee members based on seniority.[61] A committee member not given time to speak might be present in the House chamber during debate, but since he would be out of camera range, his presence would go unnoticed by a House television viewer.

The manner in which House debate assignments are made raises an especially important point regarding television viewer perception of the House. Practically every action that occurs on the House floor is a function of a very rigid and complex set of procedural rules. And in order for viewers to understand and appreciate the legislative process as practiced in the House, they first must understand the procedures that govern the process.

There are four sources of parliamentary procedure in the House: 1) the U.S. Constitution, 2) rules adopted for each new Congress, 3) rules based on the British House of Commons as compiled originally by Thomas Jefferson, and 4) previous decisions of House Speakers and Chairmen of the Committees of the Whole.[62] Digesting all that is contained in these several sources would be a formidable task for anyone. To simplify matters, guides to the more common rules and procedures have been written.[63] In addition, the Benton Foundation has published a booklet entitled *Gavel to Gavel: A Guide to the Televised Proceedings of Congress*, and the House itself has published the *Viewers' Guide to the Televised Proceedings of the U.S. House of Representatives* to aid viewers. It is essential, though, that anyone intent on learning the procedures of House deliberation study the institution's rules in conjunction with observing their application to particular situations.[64]

Limitations aside, there does exist the potential for House television to play a major role in the political socialization process. As defined by Sidney Kraus, political socialization "is the process of how we come to learn about politics, how we obtain our attitudes and values about political institutions, and how we ultimately behave politically."[65] Most American youth are cognizant of the role of government in their lives at a very early age.[66] Much of what they know has been derived from three particular "agencies of learning": the family, the formal educational system, and the mass media.[67]

While research on the subject is limited, a number of studies suggest that the media, especially television, play a political socialization role that sometimes transcends both that of the school and family.[68] The interest among many schools in providing students with access to House telecasts suggests that educators have accepted television's potential impact on political socialization. It should be noted that viewing House telecasts in a classroom situation combines two of the three major agencies of learning. Providing students with the atmosphere and the prime medium of political socialization, however, does not guarantee what effect either will have on the students. Indeed, the family still appears to be the primary determinant of how students will perceive House television and what effect the telecasts will have on them.[69]

EFFECTS OF NEW VIDEO TECHNOLOGY

New forms of video technology have emerged to provide a greater array of communication channels linking congressmen and constituents. Most of these forms fall under the category of interactive video and are new only in the sense that Congress has yet to fully embrace their capabilities. Once integrated into existing communication channels, the technology stands to profoundly affect the interrelationship between Congress and the public.

An experiment with at least one form of emerging video technology—videoconferencing—was conducted in 1977 and 1978 by the George Washington University Program of Policy Studies in Science and Technology. The program studied the feasibility of interconnecting congressional locations in Washington, D.C. with distant locations throughout the country via communications satellite. A total of twelve videoconferences were conducted, providing for the first time a convenient, cost-effective method of video interaction that ranged from constituent/congressman interviews to committee hearings.[70]

In its final report, the policy studies program staff stated,

Faced with increased complexity in social problems and the volume and diversity of citizen demands, videoconferencing can help the Congress do a better job representing the people and legislating on their behalf.

From the perspective of the public participants in the . . . experiment, videoconferencing can open up new possibilities for learning about the Congress, for acquiring more relevant information about (and participating in) the legislative process and specific issues, and for communicating views and opinions to Congress on a more timely and informed basis.[71]

The same interactive video technique that was central to the videoconferencing experiment is now possible through cable television. Several interactive cable systems in major U.S. cities allow polling of cable subscribers for opinions on key issues. Subscribers respond to questions originating at a cable television studio by pressing certain buttons on a special hand-held control unit. Conceivably, a congressman could use this system to instantaneously gather views of constituents on legislative matters. It has been suggested that polling of this kind, if perfected, has the potential of moving our nation toward a direct democracy reminiscent of the ancient Greek city-state.[72]

The technological revolution currently under way will continue to provide newer and better forms of telecommunications media, but will Congress use them? Or will the reluctance it has so often shown with television continue? Chances are that the traditions that bind Congress will evolve to a point where technology of all kinds will eventually be incorporated into the congressional environment. A Congress that continues to become more receptive to openness and a public that continues to demand greater access to its elected officials and to the legislative process in general will have much to do with that evolution. Public confidence in Congress should be a natural byproduct of congressional openness and public access. If, as predicted, television or some form of video technology yet to be invented is instrumental in creating and sustaining this confidence, it will have served Congress and the country well.

Notes

PREFACE

1. John M. Kittross and Christopher H. Sterling, *Stay Tuned: A Concise History of American Broadcasting* (Belmont, Calif.: Wadsworth Publishing Co., 1978), p. 75.
2. House Special Subcommittee on Investigations of the Committee on Interstate and Foreign Commerce, *The Fairness Doctrine and Related Issues*, 91st Cong., 1st sess., 1969, H. Rept. 91–257, p. 6.
3. Gwendolyn B. Folsom, *Legislative History: Research for the Interpretation of Laws* (Charlottesville: The University Press of Virginia, 1972), p. 1.

1. FACTORS INFLUENCING HOUSE AND SENATE TELEVISION

1. Alfred de Grazia, ed., *Congress: The First Branch of Government* (Garden City, N.Y.: Anchor Books, 1967), p. 15.
2. Ibid., p. 12.
3. Senate Subcommittee on Intergovernmental Relations, *Confidence and Concern: Citizens View American Government*, pt. 1, 93rd Cong., 1st sess., 1973, Committee Print, pp. vi-viii.
4. Congressional Research Service, *Congress and Mass Communications: An Institutional Perspective,* prepared for the Joint Committee on Congressional Operations, 93rd Cong., 2d sess., 1974, p. 1.

5. House Commission on Administrative Review, *Work of the Commission*, vol. 1, 95th Cong., 1st sess., 1977, H. Doc. 95-272.
6. Senate Subcommittee on Intergovernmental Relations, *Confidence and Concern*.
7. House Commission on Administrative Review, *Work of the Commission*, vol. 2, p. 769.
8. Ibid., pp. 816-18.
9. Ibid., pp. 818-19.
10. Glenn R. Parker and Roger H. Davidson, "Why Do Americans Love Their Congressmen So Much More Than Their Congress?" *Legislative Studies Quarterly*, 4(February 1979):58-59.
11. Richard Fenno, Jr., in *Congress in Change*, ed. Norman J. Ornstein (New York: Praeger Publishers, 1975), pp. 277-80.
12. "Congressional Unpopularity: 5 Views from the Inside," *Congressional Quarterly*, 9 March 1974, p. 600.
13. Michael J. Robinson, "Three Faces of Congressional Media," in *The New Congress*, eds. Thomas E. Mann and Norman Ornstein (Washington, D.C.: American Enterprise Institute, 1981), pp. 88-89.
14. Senate Subcommittee on Intergovernmental Relations, *Confidence and Concern*, p. 3.
15. Ibid., p. 24.
16. Congressional Research Service, *Congress and Mass Communications*, p. v.
17. House Commission on Administrative Review, *Work of the Commission*, vol. 2, p. 813.
18. Senate Subcommittee on Intergovernmental Relations, *Confidence and Concern*, p. 78.
19. House Commission on Administrative Review, *Work of the Commission*, vol. 2, p. 853.
20. Senate Subcommittee on Intergovernmental Relations, *Confidence and Concern*, p. 72.
21. National Task Force on Citizenship Education, *Education for Responsible Citizenship* (New York: McGraw-Hill Book Co., 1977), pp. 1-4.
22. Senate Subcommittee on Intergovernmental Relations, *Confidence and Concern*, pp. 78-79.
23. The Roper Organization, Inc., "Evolving Public Attitudes Toward Television and Other Mass Media, 1959-1980," (New York: Television Information Office, 1981), pp. 3-4.
24. House Commission on Administrative Review, *Work of the Commission*, vol. 2, p. 892.
25. Congressional Research Service, *Congress and Mass Communications*, p. 10.

26. Robinson, "Three Faces of Congressional Media," pp. 82–85.
27. Peter Gruenstein, "Press Release Politics: How Congressmen Manage the News," *The Progressive*, January 1974, pp. 39–40.
28. Ibid., p. 39.
29. Robinson, "Three Faces of Congressional Media," p. 63.
30. James Chamberlain, Assistant Director of Senate Recording Studio, telephone conversation with author, 9 August 1982.
31. Compiled by Edmund L. Hinshaw, Jr., Clerk of the U.S. House of Representatives, 1981.
32. U.S. House of Representatives Recording Studio Rate Schedules, introductory matter.
33. Robinson, "Three Faces of Congressional Media," p. 63.
34. Delmer Dunn, "Symbiosis: Congress and the Press," in *Congress and the News Media*, ed. Robert O. Blanchard (New York: Hastings House, Publishers, 1974), pp. 240–47.
35. Tom Littlewood, "Publicity Itch on Capitol Hill," *Saturday Review*, 13 April 1968, pp. 79–80.
36. F. B. Marbut, *News from the Capital* (Carbondale, Ill.: Southern Illinois University Press, 1971), pp. 210–19.
37. *Congressional Directory*, 97th Cong., 1st sess., 1981, pp. 880–902.
38. Executive Committee of the Congressional Radio-Television Correspondents' Galleries, *Rules and Procedures for Broadcast Coverage of Congress*, January 1982.
39. Max Barber, Superintendent, Senate Radio-Television Gallery, letter to author, 8 June 1982.
40. Len Allen, "Makeup of the Senate Press," in *Senate Communications with the Public*, 94th Cong., 2d sess., 1977, Committee Print, pp. 35–36.
41. Congressional Research Service, *Congress and Mass Communications*, pp. 64–65.
42. Ibid., p. 65.
43. Lee M. Mitchell, "Background Paper," in *Openly Arrived At*, Twentieth Century Fund Task Force on Broadcasting and the Legislature (New York: The Twentieth Century Fund, 1974), p. 67.
44. Blanchard, *Congress and the News Media*, p. 226.
45. Ibid., pp. 177, 245. See also, Michael J. Robinson and Kevin Appel, "Network News Coverage of Congress," *Political Science Quarterly*, 94(Fall 1979):412–13.
46. Mitchell, "Background Paper," p. 68.
47. George B. Galloway, *History of the House of Representatives*, revised by Sidney Wise, 2d ed. (New York: Thomas Y. Crowell Co., 1976), p. xiii.

48. House Republican Task Force on Congressional Reform and Minority Staffing, *We Propose: A Modern Congress*, ed. Mary McInnis (New York: McGraw-Hill, 1966), p. 37.
49. Charles O. Jones, "Somebody Must Be Trusted: An Essay on Leadership of the U.S. Congress," in Ornstein, *Congress in Change*, p. 268.
50. Michael Green, "Obstacles to Reform: Nobody Covers the House," *The Washington Monthly*, June 1970, p. 64.
51. Robert E. Gilbert, "Television and Political Centralization in the United States," *International Review of History and Political Science*, 12(May 1974):36–37.
52. Robert L. Peabody, Norman J. Ornstein and David W. Rohde, "The United States Senate as a Presidential Incubator: Many Are Called but Few Are Chosen," *Political Science Quarterly*, 91(Summer 1976):245.
53. Donald R. Matthews, *U.S. Senators and Their World* (Chapel Hill, N.C.: The University of North Carolina Press, 1960), p. 203.
54. Blanchard, *Congress and the News Media*, p. 177.
55. Robinson and Appel, "Network News Coverage," p. 410.
56. William C. Adams and Paul H. Ferber, "Television Interview Shows: The Politics of Visibility," *Journal of Broadcasting*, 21(Spring 1977):141–44.
57. Green, "Obstacles to Reform," p. 64.
58. See Mitchell, "Background Paper," pp. 39–45, for an excellent discussion of congressional activity related to opening committees to television coverage.
59. Nelson W. Polsby, *Congress and the Presidency*, 2d ed. (Englewood Cliffs, N.J.: Prentice-Hall, Inc., 1971), p. 95.
60. Ibid., p. 97.
61. Douglas Cater, *The Fourth Branch of Government* (Boston: Houghton Mifflin Co., 1959), p. 58.
62. Francis E. Rourke, *Secrecy and Publicity* (Baltimore: The Johns Hopkins Press, 1961), pp. 117–21.
63. Lawrence Leamer, "The Sam Ervin Show," *Harper's Magazine*, March 1972, pp. 83–85.
64. Rourke, *Secrecy and Publicity*, p. 118.
65. Ibid., p. 119.
66. Denis S. Rutkus, "Television Network News Coverage of Senate Committees," in *Operation of the Senate Committee System: Staffing, Scheduling, Communications, Procedures, and Special Functions*, Temporary Select Committee to Study the Senate Committee System, 95th Cong., 1st sess., 1977, Appendix to the Second Report, pp. 75–76.

67. Ibid., p. 77.
68. Mitchell, "Background Paper," p. 47.
69. Robinson and Appel, "Network News Coverage," p. 411.
70. Mitchell, "Background Paper," pp. 45–47.
71. James L. Sundquist, "Congress and the President: Enemies or Partners?" in *Congress Reconsidered*, eds. Lawrence C. Dodd and Bruce I. Oppenheimer (New York: Praeger Publishers, 1977), pp. 223–25.
72. Roger H. Davidson, David M. Kovenock and Michael K. O'Leary, *Congress in Crisis: Politics and Congressional Reform* (Belmont, Calif.: Wadsworth Publishing Co., 1966), pp. 12–14.
73. Clark A. Puntigam, "Television and the Congress: Preserving the Balance," *Federal Communications Bar Journal*, 26(1973):215.
74. *Columbia Broadcasting System, Inc. v. F.C.C.*, 454 F. 2d 1018, 1020 (1971).
75. Elmer E. Cornwell, Jr., *Presidential Leadership of Public Opinion* (Bloomington, Ind.: Indiana University Press, 1965), p. 4.
76. Polsby, *Congress and the Presidency*, p. 138.
77. George E. Reedy, *The Twilight of the Presidency* (New York: The World Publishing Co., 1970), pp. 41–42.
78. Elmer E. Cornwell, "The President and the Press: Phases in the Relationship," *Annals of the American Academy of Political and Social Sciences*, 427(September 1976):57.
79. Bernard Rubin, *Political Television* (Belmont, Calif.: Wadsworth Publishing Co., 1967), p. 96.
80. Newton Minow, John B. Martin and Lee M. Mitchell, *Presidential Television* (New York: Basic Books, 1973), p. 17.
81. Edward Jay Epstein, *News from Nowhere* (New York: Random House, 1973), p. 253.
82. Reedy, *The Twilight of the Presidency*, pp. 162–64.
83. House Subcommittee on Communications, *Federal Communications Commission Oversight*, 94th Cong., 2d sess., 1976, Hearings, p. 23.
84. The "equal opportunities" provisions of the Communications Act read: "If any licensee shall permit any person who is a legally qualified candidate for any public office to use a broadcasting station, he shall afford equal opportunities to all other such candidates for that office in the use of such broadcasting station." (47 U.S.C. 1191 [1976]).
85. *Aspen Institute Program on Communications*, 55 F.C.C. 2d 697, 712 (1975).
86. Ibid., p. 699.
87. Ibid., p. 698.
88. Minow, et al., *Presidential Television*, pp. 17–18.

89. House Subcommittee on Communications, *Federal Communications Commission Oversight*, pp. 26–27.
90. Ibid., p. 27.
91. Ibid., pp. 31–32. See also "Media Manipulation by the President?" *Broadcasting*, 21 October 1974, pp. 42–43.
92. David Wise, "The President and the Press," *Atlantic*, April 1973, p. 59.
93. Joint Committee on the Organization of the Congress, *Organization of Congress*, 89th Cong., 2d sess., 1966, S. Rept. 89-1414, p. 1.
94. James L. Sundquist, *The Decline and Resurgence of Congress* (Washington, D.C.: The Brookings Institution, 1981), p. 5.
95. Harvey G. Zeidenstein, "The Reassertion of Congressional Power: New Curbs on the President," *Political Science Quarterly*, 93(Fall 1978):393. See also James W. Davis and Delbert Ringquist, *The President and Congress: Toward a New Balance* (Woodbury, N.Y.: Barron's Educational Series, Inc., 1975), pp. 54–56.
96. Max M. Kampelman, "Congress, the Media and the President," *Proceedings of the Academy of Political Science*, 32(1975):88.
97. Sundquist, *The Decline and Resurgence of Congress*, pp. 35–36.
98. Lawrence C. Dodd, "Cycles of Congressional Power," *Society*, 16(November/December 1978):67.
99. "Congress Long the Object of Change and Reform," *Congressional Quarterly*, 7 June 1963, p. 859.
100. Galloway, *History of the House of Representatives*, pp. 60–61.
101. "Legislative Reorganization Act: First Year's Record," *Congressional Quarterly*, 4 March 1972, pp. 485–86.
102. Leroy N. Rieselbach, *Congressional Reform in the Seventies* (Morristown, N.J.: General Learning Press, 1977), p. 48.
103. Bruce R. Hopkins, "Congressional Reform Advances in the Ninety-third Congress," *American Bar Association Journal*, 60(January 1974):47.
104. Charles O. Jones, "Will Reform Change Congress?" in *Congress Reconsidered*, eds. Dodd and Oppenheimer, pp. 252–55.
105. Ibid., p. 255.

2. CONGRESSIONAL RADIO

1. Christopher H. Sterling and John M. Kittross, *Stay Tuned: A Concise History of American Broadcasting* (Belmont, Calif.: Wadsworth Publishing Co., 1978), pp. 58–62.

2. Gleason Archer, *History of Radio to 1926* (New York: The American Historical Society, Inc., 1938), pp. 393–97.

3. Sterling and Kittross, *Stay Tuned*, p. 62.

4. Orrin E. Dunlap, Jr., *Radio and Television Almanac* (New York: Harper & Brothers, 1951), p. 71.

5. *Congressional Record* 62 (1922) 3130.

6. *Congressional Record* 65 (1924) 5122.

7. See L. S. Howeth, *History of Communications-Electronics in the United States Navy* (Washington, D.C.: Government Printing Office, 1963), pp. 237–58, 283–96, 313–35.

8. "Message Sent by Radio," *New York Times*, 9 December 1922, p. 6.

9. Archer, *History of Radio to 1926*, p. 303.

10. *Congressional Record* 65 (1924) 5122.

11. Ibid., 7666–67.

12. Letter from the Secretary of War and Secretary of the Navy to the Senate Committee on Rules, *Broadcasting By Radio the Proceedings of the Senate*, 70th Cong., 1st sess., S. Doc. 9, pp. 2–5.

13. Mark Sullivan, "Will Radio Make the People the Government?" *Radio Broadcast*, November 1924, p. 20.

14. J. B. Morecroft, "Why Does Congress Refuse to Broadcast Its Proceedings?" *Radio Broadcast*, June 1925, pp. 198–99.

15. J. B. Morecroft, "The First Presidential Radio Inaugural," *Radio Broadcast*, May 1925, p. 37.

16. "The Voice to the People," *New York Times*, 8 December 1923, p. 12.

17. *Congressional Record* 69 (1928) 1164.

18. S.Res. 92, *Congressional Record* 69 (1928) 933; S.Res. 36, *Congressional Record* 71 (1929) 343; S.Res. 71, *Congressional Record* 75 (1931) 445; S.Res. 29, *Congressional Record* 77 (1933) 415.

19. *Congressional Record* 75 (1931) 217.

20. *Congressional Record* 81 (1937) 2196.

21. "Station Proposed for Federal Use," *New York Times*, 12 May 1929, sec. 10, p. 21.

22. "Radio Gets Taste of Congress," *New York Times*, 11 December 1932, sec. 8, p. 6.

23. Alan Brinkley, *Voices of Protest* (New York: Alfred A. Knopf, 1982), p. 62.

24. Edward W. Chester, *Radio, Television and American Politics* (New York: Sheed and Ward, 1969), pp. 62–63.

25. Statement of Paul Sifton, Director, Washington Bureau of the Union for Democratic Action in Joint Committee on the Organiza-

tion of Congress, *Organization of Congress*, pt. 4, 79th Cong., 1st sess., 1945, Hearings, p. 937.

26. Ibid., pp. 938–40.
27. Hadley Cantril, ed., *Public Opinion, 1935–1946* (Princeton, N.J.: Princeton University Press, 1951), pp. 712–13.
28. Sifton in Joint Committee on the Organization of Congress, *Organization of Congress*, p. 941.
29. *Congressional Record* 90 (1944) 6931.
30. "Congress on the Air?" *Time*, 9 October 1944, p. 75.
31. *Congressional Record* 93 (1947) 166.
32. *Congressional Record* 90 (1944) 9536–40.
33. Joint Committee on the Organization of Congress, *Organization of Congress*, p. 63.
34. Ibid., pp. 220, 1077.
35. Ibid., pp. 83–85.
36. Ibid., p. 940.
37. Ibid., p. 325.
38. Pub. L. 79–601 (2 August 1946) 60 Stat. 812.
39. Robert E. Summers, "The Role of Congressional Broadcasting in a Democratic Society" (Ph.D. diss., The Ohio State University, 1955), pp. 213–14.
40. Erik Barnouw, *Tube of Plenty* (New York: Oxford University Press, 1975), pp. 99–103.
41. "Television Is Used at House Opening," *New York Times*, 4 January 1947, p. 2.

3. TELEVISING CONGRESSIONAL HEARINGS

1. Ralph Goldman, "Congress on the Air," *Public Opinion Quarterly*, 14(1950):744.
2. "Congressional Investigations," *Guide to Congress*, 2d ed. (Washington, D.C.: Congressional Quarterly, Inc., 1976), pp. 142–43.
3. Ibid., p. 141.
4. "Trial by Congress," *Senior Scholastic*, 24 October 1951, p. 8.
5. Senate Committee on Rules and Administration, *Reform in Procedure Before Congressional Committees*, 81st Cong., 1st sess., 1949, Hearings, p. 2.
6. Legislative Reference Service, "References to Congressional Committee Hearings Televised or Photographed by Newsreel Cameras

and Committees That Have Restricted the Use of These Media," in *Congressional Record* 98 (1952) A2836–37.

7. "Who's a Liar," *Life*, 2 April 1951, p. 22.

8. Ronald Garay, "Television and the 1951 Senate Crime Committee Hearings," *Journal of Broadcasting*, 22(Fall 1978):469–72.

9. "Crime Hearings," *Broadcasting/Telecasting*, 26 February 1951, p. 56.

10. Garay, "Television and the 1951 Senate Crime Committee Hearings," pp. 476–79.

11. Ibid., pp. 481–85.

12. *United States v. Kleinman et al.*, 107 F. Supp. 407 (1952).

13. *Congressional Record* 97 (1951) 9766.

14. Ibid., p. 3040.

15. Ibid., pp. 9137–38.

16. Ibid., p. 9768.

17. Ibid., pp. 9773–74.

18. Ibid., p. 9792.

19. Ibid., p. 9777.

20. Ibid., p. 9783.

21. Ibid., pp. 9802–3.

22. See for example, Thurman Arnold, "Mob Justice and Television," *Journal of the Federal Communications Bar Association*, 12(Spring/Summer 1951):4–9; William T. Gossett, "Justice and TV: Some Thoughts on Congressional Investigations," *American Bar Association Journal*, 38(January 1952):15–18+; Virgil C. McClintock, "Congressional Inquisition by Television," *Oklahoma Law Review*, 5(May 1952):230–39; Joseph M. Snee, "One for the Money, Two for the Show: The Case Against Televising Congressional Hearings," *Georgetown Law Journal*, 42(November 1953):1–43; Telford Taylor, "The Issue Is Not TV, But Fair Play," *Journal of the Federal Communications Bar Association*, 12(Spring/Summer 1951):10–15; "Television and Congressional Investigations," *DePaul Law Review*, 1(Autumn/Winter 1951):112–20; Paul J. Yesawich, Jr., "Televising and Broadcasting Trials," *Cornell Law Quarterly*, 37(1952):701–17.

23. See for example, articles and editorials appearing in various U.S. newspapers and magazines as reprinted in *Congressional Record* 97 (1951) 9796–9801.

24. Gossett, "Justice and TV," p. 16.

25. Edward Bennett Williams, *One Man's Freedom* (New York: Atheneum, 1962), p. 230.

26. McClintock, "Congressional Inquisition by Television," p. 235.

27. George B. Galloway, "Congressional Investigations: Proposed

Reforms," *University of Chicago Law Review,* 18(Spring 1951):480–83.

28. Excellent portraits of the House Committee on Un-American Activities are available in Eric Bentley, ed., *Thirty Years of Treason* (New York: The Viking Press, 1971) and Walter Goodman, *The Committee* (New York: Farrar, Straus, and Giroux, 1968).

29. Senate Committee on Rules and Administration, *Reform in Procedure Before Congressional Committees,* pp. 11–28, 38, 43–46, 54–57, 91–97, 98–101.

30. Ibid., p. 9.

31. Ibid.

32. Taylor, "The Issue Is Not TV," p. 11.

33. Jack Gould, "Major Issues Seen in Telecasts Now," *New York Times,* 23 March 1951, p. 12.

34. Richard Rovere, "Television in Courts and Legislatures," in *The Eighth Art* (New York: Holt, Rinehart and Winston, 1962), pp. 136–37.

35. Abiah A. Church and Vincent T. Wasilewski, "Televising Legislative Hearings," *The Federal Bar Journal,* 14(January/March 1954):63.

36. "Television and Congressional Investigations," p. 114.

37. Williams, *One Man's Freedom,* p. 229.

38. Rovere, "Television in Courts and Legislatures," p. 138.

39. *Allen B. Dumont Laboratories v. Carroll,* 184 F. 2d 153, 156 (1950).

40. Eugene G. Partain, "The Use of Broadcast Media in Congressional, Legislative and Quasi-Judicial Proceedings," *Journal of Broadcasting,* 4(Spring 1960):127.

41. Samuel I. Shuman, *Broadcasting and Telecasting of Judicial and Legislative Proceedings* (Ann Arbor, Mich.: University of Michigan Legislative Research Center, 1956), p. 5.

42. McClintock, "Congressional Inquisition by Television," p. 234.

43. Ibid., pp. 238–39.

44. Shuman, *Broadcasting and Telecasting,* p. 80.

45. Snee, "One for the Money," pp. 17–18.

46. *United States v. Kleinman et al.,* 107 F. Supp. 407, 408 (1952).

47. See Henry J. Merry, "The Investigating Power of Congress: Its Scope and Limitations," *American Bar Association Journal,* 40(December 1954):1073–76+. The matter of televised effects on witnesses appearing before the Kefauver Committee arose in other court cases. Although the central issues of each case differed considerably from *Kleinman,* the decision in one, *United States v. Orman,* 207 F.

Notes

2d 148 (1953), cited *Kleinman* directly (p. 158). The second case, *U.S. v. Moran*, 194 F. 2d 623 (1952), was decided prior to *Kleinman*. The defendant Moran argued that his perjury conviction should have been reversed by the U.S. Court of Appeals because, in part, the presence of television cameras, microphones, etc. adversely affected hearing decorum and thus the tribunal's competence. Judge Thomas Swann wrote in the court's affirmation of the conviction, "Opinions may differ as to whether such procedure is better calculated to achieve publicity for the investigators than to promote their investigations. But on the record before us no facts have been proved which would justify holding that the tribunal was incompetent" (p. 627).

48. See Senate Committee on Expenditures in the Executive Departments, *Organization and Operation of Congress*, 82d Cong., 1st sess., 1951, Hearings, p. 136.

49. Church and Wasilewski, "Televising Legislative Hearings," p. 66. This point has been underscored by others who suggested that newsreel cameras, not television cameras, were the ones requiring excessive lights, and those operating the newsreel cameras were generally the source of the noise. The point was made that television cameras actually required no more than the natural light in a hearing room to function and that they could be concealed behind a screen. Comments of Ralph Hardy, "Is Radio-TV Exclusion from Government Hearings Justified," *Town Meeting*, 24 August 1954, pp. 3–4.

50. *Barsky v. United States*, 167 F. 2d 241, 250 (1948).

51. Taylor, "The Issue Is Not TV," p. 12.

52. Alan Barth, *Government by Investigation* (New York: The Viking Press, 1955), p. 71.

53. Yesawich, "Televising and Broadcasting Trials," p. 703.

54. Arnold, "Mob Justice and Television," p. 6.

55. Richard H. Rovere, *Senator Joe McCarthy* (New York: World Publishing, 1973), pp. 122–25.

56. Ibid., p. 24.

57. J. Fred MacDonald, *Don't Touch That Dial!* (Chicago: Nelson-Hall, 1979), p. 321. For a thorough discussion of hearings and other activity related to the McCarthy era see Arthur M. Schlesinger, Jr., and Roger Bruns, eds., *Congress Investigates: A Documented History, 1792–1974* (New York: Chelsea House, 1975), 5:3729–3919; and Michael Straight, *Trial by Television* (Boston: The Beacon Press, 1954).

58. Robert E. Summers, "The Role of Congressional Broadcasting in a Democratic Society" (Ph.D. diss., The Ohio State University, 1955), 230–33.

59. Edward Bliss, Jr., ed., *In Search of Light: The Broadcasts of Edward R. Murrow, 1938–1961* (New York: Avon, 1967), p. 265.
60. Edward W. Chester, *Radio, Television and American Politics* (New York: Sheed and Ward, 1969), pp. 94–95.
61. Galloway, "Congressional Investigations," pp. 482–83.
62. Senate Committee on Rules and Administration, *Reform in Procedure Before Congressional Committees*, p. 9.
63. Ibid., pp. 11–28, 38, 43–46, 91–101.
64. Galloway listed some forty-one distinct items to be included in a code of standards as suggested in numerous bills and resolutions introduced on the subject. Galloway, "Congressional Investigations," pp. 496–98.
65. Senate Committee on Expenditures in the Executive Departments, *Organization and Operation of Congress*, p. 132.
66. Galloway, "Congressional Investigations," pp. 490–92.
67. Senate Special Committee to Investigate Organized Crime in Interstate Commerce, *Organized Crime in Interstate Commerce*, 82d Cong., lst sess., 1951, S. Rept. 725, p. 101.
68. Senate Special Committee to Investigate Organized Crime in Interstate Commerce, *Third Interim Report*, 82d Cong., lst sess., 1951, S. Rept. 307, p. 25.
69. Senate Special Committee to Investigate Organized Crime in Interstate Commerce, *Organized Crime in Interstate Commerce*, pp. 99–103.
70. "The Congressional Investigation—Its Authority, Record, Procedures, Future," *Congressional Digest*, May 1952, pp. 143–44.
71. "Broadcasting and Telecasting of Trials and Hearings: Bar Association Views," *Journal of the Federal Communications Bar Association*, 12(Autumn 1952):226–27.
72. "American Civil Liberties Union Statement on Filming, Broadcasting and Televising of Courtroom Proceeding, Legislative Sessions and Legislative Hearings," *Journal of the Federal Communications Bar Association*, 13(Spring 1953):8–10. See also statement by M. S. Novik, "Telecasting Legislative Hearings," in *Education on the Air*, ed. O. Joe Olson, 23d Yearbook of Institute for Education by Radio and Television, The Ohio State University, 1953, pp. 49–51.
73. Senate Subcommittee on Rules, *Rules of Procedure for Senate Investigating Committees*, 83d Cong., 2d sess., 1954, Hearings, pp. 12–13.
74. Ibid., pp. 1–9.
75. Ibid., pts. 1–10.

76. Senate Committee on Rules and Administration, *Rules of Procedure for Senate Investigating Committees*, 84th Cong., 1st sess., 1955, S. Rept. 2, pp. 28–31.
77. Broadcasting and Telecasting of Congressional Committee Hearings," *Journal of the Federal Communications Bar Association*, 14(1955):136–37.
78. *Congressional Record* 98 (1952) 1334–35.
79. Ibid., p. A1519.
80. Ibid., p. A1874.
81. Ibid., p. A1519.
82. Ibid., p. 1568.
83. David Halberstam, *The Powers That Be* (New York: Alfred A. Knopf, 1979), pp. 245–46.
84. Summers, "The Role of Congressional Broadcasting," pp. 220–21.
85. "Rayburn Bans House TV Shows," *Broadcasting/Telecasting*, 3 January 1955, pp. 46–48.
86. *Congressional Record* 101 (1955) 494.
87. Ibid., p. 628.
88. Ibid., p. 794.
89. "House Unit Blocks Move to Allow Broadcast Coverage," *Broadcasting/Telecasting*, 14 March 1955, p. 84.
90. "House Hearing Aired in California," *Broadcasting/Telecasting*, 24 June 1957, p. 68.
91. Warren Unna, "Walter Scorns Rayburn's House Rule, Continues Televising His Hearing," *Washington Post*, 21 June 1957, p. A1.
92. *Congressional Record* 107 (1961) 2305.
93. "Access to House Hearings Is Doubtful," *Broadcasting*, 11 March 1963, p. 80.
94. *Congressional Record* 107 (1961) 2610.
95. *Congressional Record* 108 (1962) 267–68.
96. "McCormack Noncommittal on House Radio-TV Coverage," *Broadcasting*, 8 January 1962, p. 50.
97. *Congressional Record* 108 (1962) 223–27.
98. Ibid., pp. 267–69.
99. "Meader Fails to Beat Ban," *Broadcasting*, 22 January 1962, p. 48.
100. Shuman, *Broadcasting and Telecasting*, p. 60.
101. Summers, "The Role of Congressional Broadcasting," pp. 240–41.

4. TELEVISION COVERS HOUSE COMMITTEES AND WATERGATE INVESTIGATIONS

1. *Congressional Record* 111 (1965) 4340.
2. John F. Bibby and Roger H. Davidson, *On Capitol Hill*, 2d ed. (Hinsdale, Ill.: Dryden Press, 1972), pp. 252–54.
3. *Congressional Record* 111 (1965) 4340.
4. Joint Committee on the Organization of the Congress, *Organization of Congress*, 89th Cong., 2d sess., 1966, S. Rept. 89–1414, p. 3.
5. Joint Committee on the Organization of the Congress, *Organization of Congress*, 89th Cong., 2d sess., 1966, S. Rept. 89–948, pp. 28–29.
6. Joint Committee on the Organization of the Congress, *Organization of Congress*, pt. 7, 89th Cong., 1st sess., 1965, Hearings, pp. 1041–42.
7. Ibid., pt. 1, pp. 36–37.
8. Ibid., pt. 3, p. 496.
9. Ibid., pt. 10, p. 1496.
10. Roger H. Davidson, David Kovenock and Michael O'Leary, "Congressional Reorganization: Problems and Prospects" (Paper prepared for the Orvil E. Dryfoos Conference on Public Affairs, Dartmouth College, 7, 8 March 1964), in Joint Committee on the Organization of the Congress, *Organization of Congress,* pt. 5, Hearings, pp. 760–61.
11. Joint Committee on the Organization of the Congress, *Organization of Congress*, S. Rept. 89–1414, pp. 10–11.
12. Ibid., pp. 45–48.
13. Ibid., p. 57.
14. "First Congressional Reform Bill Enacted Since 1946," *Congressional Quarterly Almanac* (Washington, D.C.: Congressional Quarterly, Inc., 1970), p. 451.
15. Ibid.
16. House Special Subcommittee on Legislative Reorganization, *Legislative Reorganization Act of 1970*, 91st Cong., 1st sess., 1969, Hearings, pp. 35–36.
17. Ibid., pp. 85–86.
18. Ibid., pp. 64–65.
19. House Committee on Rules, *Legislative Reorganization Act of 1970*, 91st Cong., 2d sess., 1970, H. Rept. 91–1215, pp. 6–7.
20. *Congressional Record* 116 (1970) 24970–76.
21. Ibid., pp. 32309–10.

22. Ibid., p. 35048.
23. Ibid., pp. 35838–42.
24. 84 stat. 1140. Bibby and Davidson, *On Capitol Hill*, provide an excellent analysis of the six-year political evolution of P.L. 91–510, pp. 251–80.
25. 84 stat. 1187.
26. Norman J. Ornstein, ed., *Congress in Change* (New York: Praeger Publishers, Inc., 1975), p. 199.
27. Newton Minow, John B. Martin and Lee M. Mitchell, *Presidential Television* (New York: Basic Books, 1973), p. 69.
28. *Fairness Doctrine Ruling*, 25 FCC 2d 283, 285–86 (1970).
29. Minow, et al., *Presidential Television*, pp. 118–19.
30. *Fairness Doctrine Ruling*, pp. 285–86.
31. Ibid., p. 294.
32. Ibid., pp. 296–97.
33. David Halberstam, *The Powers That Be* (New York: Alfred A. Knopf, 1979), pp. 492–96.
34. Ibid., pp. 503–7. See also, Fred Friendly, *Due to Circumstances Beyond Our Control* (New York: Vintage Books, 1968), pp. 212–65.
35. Senate Communications Subcommittee, *Public Service Time for the Legislative Branch*, 91st Cong., 2d sess., 1970, Hearings, pp. 9–10.
36. Ibid., p. 15.
37. Ibid., pp. 51–52.
38. Ibid., pp. 102–4.
39. Ibid., pp. 34–35.
40. Ibid., p. 83.
41. Ibid., pp. 124–25.
42. "Chance to Open Congress to Cameras?" *Broadcasting*, 10 August 1970, pp. 19–25.
43. Editorial, "The Right Kind of Access," *Broadcasting*, 10 August 1970, p. 66.
44. Senate Communications Subcommittee, *Public Service Time for the Legislative Branch*, p. 10.
45. Philip B. Kurland, "The Watergate Inquiry, 1973," in *Congress Investigates*, eds. Arthur M. Schlesinger, Jr. and Roger Bruns (New York: Chelsea House Publishers, 1975), 5:3923.
46. Ibid., p. 3925.
47. Ibid., p. 3926.
48. *Congressional Record* 119 (1973) 3849.
49. Kurland, "The Watergate Inquiry, 1973," pp. 3926–27.

50. As quoted in Kurland, "The Watergate Inquiry, 1973, " p. 3930.
51. "300-plus Hours of Watergate Cost Networks Up to $10 Million," *Broadcasting*, 13 August 1973, p. 15.
52. *Watergate: Chronology of a Crisis* (Washington, D.C.: Congressional Quarterly, Inc., 1975), p. 532.
53. Michael Robinson, "The Impact of the Televised Watergate Hearings," *Journal of Communication*, 24(Spring 1974):17.
54. "300-plus Hours of Watergate," pp. 15–18.
55. Ben Bagdikian, "Newspapers: Learning (Too Slowly) to Adapt to TV," *Columbia Journalism Review*, 12(November/December 1973):46.
56. *The Gallup Poll, Public Opinion 1972–1977* (Wilmington, Delaware: Scholarly Resources, Inc., 1978), 1:158–60.
57. Kurland, "The Watergate Inquiry, 1973," p. 3932.
58. *Congressional Record* 119 (1973) 28647–48.
59. *Watergate: Chronology of a Crisis*, p. 532.
60. "300-plus Hours of Watergate," p. 18.
61. Robinson, "The Impact of the Televised Watergate Hearings," pp. 17–21.
62. *Watergate: Chronology of a Crisis*, p. 111.
63. James Hamilton, *The Power to Probe* (New York: Random House, 1976), p. 20.
64. *Watergate: Chronology of a Crisis*, p. 111.
65. Hamilton, *The Power to Probe*, p. 22.
66. Ibid., pp. 45–47.
67. Ibid., pp. 53–55.
68. Senate Select Committee on Presidential Campaign Activities, *The Final Report*, 93d Cong., 2d sess., 1974, S. Rept. 93–981, pp. XXXI-XXXII.
69. House Committee on the Judiciary, *Impeachment of Richard M. Nixon, President of the United States*, 93d Cong., 2d sess., 1974, H. Rept. 93–1305, pp. 6–11.
70. *Watergate: Chronology of a Crisis*, p. 713.
71. House Committee on Rules, *Amending the Rules of the House of Representatives to Provide for the Broadcasting of Meetings, in Addition to Hearings, of House Committees Which Are Open to the Public*, 93d Cong., 2d sess., 1974, H. Rept. 93–1207.
72. *Congressional Record* 120 (daily ed., 22 July 1974) H6803–14.
73. Paul Harris, "Television Gets Its Nixon Spectacular," *Variety*, 24 July 1974, pp. 33 + .
74. "Historic Coverage for Historic Events," *Broadcasting*, 29 July 1974, pp. 29–30.

75. "Nixon's Days in Court Are TV's Too; Impeachment Coverage Makes History," *Broadcasting*, 5 August 1974, pp. 21-22.
76. John J. O'Connor, "TV: Verdict on Impeachment Coverage? Justified," *New York Times*, 29 July 1974, p. 47.
77. *The Gallup Poll, Public Opinion* 1972-1977, 1:346-47.
78. Ibid., p. 256.
79. *Congressional Record* 119 (1973) 42724-25.
80. Congressional Research Service, *Congress and Mass Communications: An Institutional Perspective*, prepared for the Joint Committee on Congressional Operations, 93d Cong., 2d sess., 1974, p. v.
81. Ibid., pp. 44-46.
82. Ibid., pp. 48-56.
83. Ibid., pp. 57-58.
84. Joint Committee on Congressional Operations, *Congress and Mass Communications*, 93d Cong., 2d sess., 1974, Hearings, p. 2.
85. Ibid., pp. 11-17.
86. Ibid., p. 4.
87. Ibid., p. 88.
88. Ibid., pp. 331-32.
89. Ibid., p. 219.
90. Ibid., pp. 227-31.
91. Ibid., pp. 404-19.
92. Joint Committee on Congressional Operations, *Broadcasting House and Senate Proceedings*, 93d Cong., 2d sess., 1974, S. Rept. 93-1275, pp. 1-2.
93. Ibid., pp. 53-56.
94. Joint Committee on Congressional Operations, *A Clear Message to the People*, 94th Cong., 1st sess., 1975, S. Rept. 94-419, p. 3.
95. See *Congressional Record* 120 (1974) 38824-28, for remarks on introduction of S. Res. 447.
96. "Two for the Books," *Broadcasting*, 23 December 1974, p. 8.

5. CONGRESS CONSIDERS CHAMBER TELEVISION

1. *Congressional Record* 121 (daily ed., 28 January 1975) S1073-74.
2. *Congressional Record* 121 (daily ed., 6 June 1975) S9972-76.
3. *Congressional Record* 121 (daily ed., 9 June 1975) S10148-149.
4. *Congressional Record* 121 (daily ed., 10 June 1975) S10301.

5. "Didn't They Almost Make It This Time?" *Broadcasting*, 16 June 1975, p. 43.
6. *Congressional Record* 121 (daily ed., 11 June 1975) S10425-26.
7. Commission on the Operation of the Senate, *Senate Communications with the Public*, 94th Cong., 2d sess., 1977, Committee Print.
8. Len Allen, "Television from the Senate Floor," in Commission on the Operation of the Senate, *Senate Communications with the Public*, p. 87.
9. Allen, "Television from the Senate Floor," pp. 97-103.
10. Commission on the Operation of the Senate, *Toward a Modern Senate*, 94th Cong., 2d sess., 1976, S. Doc. 94-278, pp. 67-68.
11. *Congressional Record* 121 (daily ed., 14 April 1975) E1722.
12. "Hill Broadcast Test Draws Support, Fire," *Broadcasting*, 21 April 1975, p. 47.
13. Michael Barone, Grant Ujifusa and Douglas Matthews, *The Almanac of American Politics* (Boston: Gambit, 1974), pp. 90-91.
14. John F. Bibby and Roger H. Davidson, *On Capitol Hill*, 2d ed. (Hinsdale, Illinois: The Dryden Press, Inc., 1972), pp. 261-62.
15. Barone, et al., *The Almanac of American Politics*, pp. 230-32; 264-66.
16. Ibid., pp. 106-7.
17. Ted Vaden, "Congress on TV: Who Will Control the Camera?" *Congressional Quarterly*, 26 April 1975, pp. 868-70.
18. Frank Jordan, Chairman, Network Pool, letter reprinted in House Ad Hoc Subcommittee on Broadcasting, *Television and Radio Coverage of the House*, 94th Cong., 1st sess., 1975, Hearings, pp. 84-85.
19. House Ad Hoc Subcommittee on Broadcasting, *Broadcast Coverage of House Floor Proceedings*, An Explanation of H. Res. 875 and Comparison with H. Res. 269, 94th Cong., 1st sess., 1975, Committee Print, pp. 1-14.
20. House Ad Hoc Subcommittee on Broadcasting, *Television and Radio Coverage of the House*, Hearings, pp. 9-10.
21. House Ad Hoc Subcommittee on Broadcasting, *Broadcast Coverage of House Floor Proceedings*, Report, 94th Cong., 2d sess., 1976, Committee Print, p. 4.
22. Ibid., pp. 19-20.
23. "More Obstacles Pop Up as Broadcasting in the House Takes a Step Forward," *Broadcasting*, 9 February 1976, p. 36.
24. House Ad Hoc Subcommittee on Broadcasting, *Broadcast Coverage of House Floor Proceedings*, Supplemental Report, 94th Cong., 2d sess., 1976, Committee Print, pp. 1-2.

25. Bruce F. Freed, "House Leadership Opposes Broadcast Plan," *Congressional Quarterly*, 20 March 1976, p. 623.
26. House Committee on Rules, *Television and Radio Coverage of the House*, 94th Cong., 2d sess., 1976, Hearings, pp. 12–17.
27. Ibid., p. 41.
28. Ibid., p. 37.
29. Ibid., pp. 56–64.
30. House Ad Hoc Subcommittee on Broadcasting, *Broadcast Coverage of House Floor Proceedings*, Second Supplemental Report, 94th Cong., 2d sess., 1976, Committee Print, p. 2.
31. *Congressional Record* 122 (daily ed., 25 May 1976) E2826.
32. House Ad Hoc Subcommittee on Broadcasting, *Broadcast Coverage of House Floor Proceedings*, Second Supplemental Report, pp. 4–6.
33. Ibid., p. 22.
34. Ibid., p. 27.
35. "Broadcasting in the House: Sisk Refuses to Let It Die," *Broadcasting*, 7 June 1976, p. 45.
36. *Congressional Record* 123 (daily ed., 24 September 1977) S15587–88.
37. Senate Committee on Rules and Administration, *Providing for Radio Coverage of the Proceedings of the Senate During Consideration of the Panama Canal Treaties*, 95th Cong., 2d sess., 1978, S. Rept. 95–630.
38. *Congressional Record* 124 (daily ed., 2 February 1978) S1102.
39. "Radio Is Pro Tem in the Senate for Canal Debates," *Broadcasting*, 13 February 1978, pp. 27–28.
40. "Panama Canal Coverage Scores for NPR Stations," *Broadcasting*, 20 February 1978, pp. 60–61.
41. Editorial, "The Sound of the Senate," *Washington Post*, 14 February 1978, p. A18.
42. *Congressional Record* 124 (daily ed., 6 April 1978) S4930–31.
43. Office of the Speaker, U.S. House of Representatives, Press Release, 2 March 1977.
44. *Congressional Record* 123 (daily ed., 8 March 1977) H1851–53.
45. John Carmody, "When We Last Left the House Speaker . . .," *Washington Post*, 16 March 1977, p. B1.
46. *Congressional Record* 123 (daily ed., 15 March 1977) H2070–75.
47. House Select Committee on Congressional Operations, *Televising the House*, 95th Cong., 1st sess., 1977, H. Doc. 95–231, pp. 13–21.

48. Ibid., pp. 23–29.
49. Ibid., pp. 3–8.
50. *Congressional Record* 123 (daily ed., 27 October 1977) H11679.
51. *Congressional Record* 123 (daily ed., 20 October 1977) H11390–91.
52. Ibid.
53. House Committee on Rules, *Providing for Radio and Television Coverage of House Proceedings*, 95th Cong., 1st sess., 1977, H. Rept. 95–759.
54. *Congressional Record* 123 (daily ed., 27 October 1977) H11679.
55. See Ann Cooper, "House Gets Set to Televise Sessions with Its Own Hand on the Cameras," *Congressional Quarterly*, 17 December 1977, p. 2605. See also, "House Members to Get Their Say on TV Control of Proceedings," *Broadcasting*, 30 January 1978, p. 38.
56. *Congressional Record* 123 (daily ed., 27 October 1977) H11678–90.
57. John Anderson, "The House on TV: Who Should Control the Cameras?" *Washington Post*, 19 January 1978, p. A25.
58. B. F. Sisk, "Controlling TV Cameras on Capitol Hill," *New York Times*, 11 February 1978, p. 21.
59. Editorial, "Not-So-Candid Camera in the House," *New York Times*, 10 January 1978, p. 32.
60. Editorial, "Better Way," *Broadcasting*, 13 February 1978, p. 130.
61. "House Members to Get Their Say," p. 38.
62. *Congressional Record* 124 (daily ed., 9 February 1978) H850. See also, *Congressional Record* 124 (daily ed., 14 June 1978) H5560.
63. Ann Cooper, "House Television Coverage Won't Begin This Year," *Congressional Quarterly*, 11 February 1978, p. 347.
64. House Committee on Rules, *Broadcasting the Proceedings of the House*, 95th Cong., 2d sess., 1978, H. Rept. 95–881, pp. 5–11.
65. Ibid., pp. 9–11.
66. James Jerome, Speaker of the Canadian House of Commons, unpublished interview, Ottawa, Canada, 29 January 1978. Transcript provided by Tom Van Dusen, Special Adviser to the Speaker.
67. House Committee on Rules, *Broadcasting the Proceedings of the House*, pp. 11–15.
68. Ann Cooper, "Canada's New TV Hit: The House of Commons," *Congressional Quarterly*, 7 January 1978, p. 24.
69. James Jerome, unpublished interview, p. 12.
70. House Committee on Rules, *Broadcasting the Proceedings of the House*, pp. 16–18.
71. "Radio and Television Broadcasting of the Proceedings of the

House of Commons of Canada," unpublished report provided by Tom Van Dusen, Special Adviser to the Speaker of the House of Commons, pp. 4–8.

72. *Congressional Record* 124 (daily ed., 7 February 1978) H770–71

73. "Hope Fades for Broadcast Control of House Cameras," *Broadcasting*, 6 February 1978, pp. 31–32.

74. National News Council Report, "Statement on Cameras in the House," *Columbia Journalism Review*, 16(March/April 1978):76.

75. *Congressional Record* 124 (daily ed., 8 June 1978) H5134.

76. "Radio Gets to Pick Up House, Not Cover It," *Broadcasting*, 12 June 1978, p. 42.

77. "Open House," *Broadcasting*, 19 June 1978, p. 50.

78. *Congressional Record* 124 (daily ed., 14 June 1978) H5553.

79. Ibid., pp. H5559–70.

6. TELEVISION ENTERS THE HOUSE WHILE THE SENATE DELAYS THE INEVITABLE

1. *Congressional Record* 125 (daily ed., 15 January 1979) H5.
2. Ibid., p. H13.
3. *Congressional Record* 125 (daily ed., 18 January 1979) E111.
4. Editorial, "Your Congressman on Tape," *Washington Post*, 17 January 1979, p. A12.
5. *Congressional Record* 125 (daily ed., 18 January 1979) E112.
6. Ann Cooper, "Curtain Rising on House TV Amid Aid-to-Incumbent Fears," *Congressional Quarterly*, 10 February 1979, pp. 253–54.
7. *Congressional Record* 125 (daily ed., 18 January 1979) E112.
8. Cooper, "Curtain Rising on House TV," p. 254.
9. Ibid., p. 253.
10. *Congressional Record* 125 (daily ed., 19 March 1979) H1427.
11. Inside Congress Notes, "House TV Coverage," *Congressional Quarterly*, 24 March 1979, p. 516.
12. "House Blacks Out Votes as Coverage by Cameras Begins," *Broadcasting*, 26 March 1979, p. 102.
13. Advertisement, *Washington Post*, 19 March 1979, p. B9.
14. "House Blacks Out Votes," p. 102.
15. Inside Congress Notes, "House TV Coverage," *Congressional Quarterly*, 7 April 1979, p. 637.
16. Norman Black, "Cable Services Threaten Public Affairs Network," *Baton Rouge Morning Advocate*, 22 March 1982, p. 10-A.

17. Joan Teague, Director, House Broadcasting System, interview with author, Washington, D.C., 14 June 1979.
18. Charlie Rose, Member, U.S. House of Representatives, letter to House colleagues, 14 March 1979.
19. Edmund L. Henshaw, Jr., Clerk, U.S. House of Representatives, letter to House members, 20 March 1979.
20. See Tape Duplication Form, Office of Records and Registration, Longworth House Office Building, Washington, D.C.
21. Irwin Arieff, "Few House TV Tapes Sold; Cost, Political Fears Cited," *Congressional Quarterly*, 5 May 1979, p. 829.
22. "C-SPAN Outtakes Used As Campaign Ammunition," *Broadcasting*, 1 November 1982, p. 50.
23. Ibid., p. 51.
24. Inside Congress Notes, "House Television System," *Congressional Quarterly*, 2 February 1980, p. 280.
25. "Television System in House Viewed as Election Threat by Some House Incumbents," *Congressional Quarterly*, 19 January 1980, p. 144.
26. "C-SPAN Caught in Political Tussle," *Broadcasting*, 10 January 1983, p. 95.
27. Ibid.
28. Inside Congress Notes, "House TV Coverage," p. 516.
29. "House Blacks Out Votes," p. 102.
30. *Congressional Record* 125 (daily ed., 15 October 1979) S14549.
31. *Congressional Record* 127 (daily ed., 6 January 1981) S121.
32. "Survey Shows: 57 Senators Give Support to Telecasting Proceedings," *Congressional Quarterly*, 7 March 1981, p. 430.
33. Senate Committee on Rules and Administration, *Television and Radio Coverage of Proceedings in the Senate Chamber*, 97th Cong., 1st sess., 1981, Hearings, p. 2.
34. Ibid., pp. 3–7.
35. Ibid., pp. 26–27.
36. Ibid., pp. 73–79.
37. Ibid., pp. 136–43.
38. Ibid., p. 16.
39. Pete Howard, Vice President, Imero Fiorentino Associates, Inc., letter to John Sweringen, 1 May 1981, in Senate Committee on Rules and Administration, *Television and Radio Coverage of Proceedings in the Senate Chamber*, p. 269.
40. Senate Committee on Rules and Administration, *Television and Radio Coverage of Proceedings in the Senate Chamber*, pp. 16, 21–23.
41. Ibid., pp. 61–65.

42. Ibid., p. 249.
43. Senate Committee on Rules and Administration, *Television and Radio Coverage of Proceedings in the Senate Chamber*, 97th Cong., 1st sess., 1981, S. Rept. 97–178, pp. 7–8.
44. Ibid., pp. 1–6.
45. *Congressional Record* 128 (daily ed., 2 February 1982) S269.
46. Ibid., p. S271.
47. Ibid., p. S280.
48. *Congressional Record* 128 (daily ed., 3 February 1982) S348.
49. *Congressional Record* 128 (daily ed., 8 February 1982) S453.
50. *Congressional Record* 128 (daily ed., 3 February 1982) S347.
51. *Congressional Record* 128 (daily ed., 2 February 1982) S283.
52. *Congressional Record* 128 (daily ed., 4 February 1982) S415.
53. "TV in Senate: Baker Fears It's Slipping Away," *Broadcasting*, 15 February 1982, p. 34.
54. *Congressional Record* 128 (daily ed., 8 February 1982) S455.
55. "Closing In on S. Res. 20," *Broadcasting*, 19 April 1982, p. 27.
56. Ibid.
57. *Congressional Record* 128 (daily ed., 20 April 1982) S3691.
58. "Catch–82: Senate's Approval of TV Coverage," *Broadcasting*, 28 April 1982, p. 32.
59. *Congressional Record* 128 (daily ed., 21 April 1982) S3798.
60. Ibid.
61. Ibid., pp. S3803–4.
62. Senate Committee on Rules and Administration, *Regulations to Implement Television and Radio Coverage of Senate Proceedings*, 97th Cong., 2d sess., 1982, S. Rept. 97–506, p. 2.
63. "TV in Senate Put on Hold," *Broadcasting*, 5 July 1982, p. 61.
64. Senate Committee on Rules and Administration, *Regulations to Implement Television and Radio Coverage of Senate Proceedings*, pp. 13, 15–16.
65. Ibid., pp. 13–14.
66. Ibid. p. 3.
67. *Congressional Record* 128 (daily ed., 27 July 1982)S9234–35.
68. "TV in Senate Vote Last in '82 Line," *Broadcasting*, 26 July 1982, p. 102.
69. David Lawsky, "Baker Still Expects Win for Senate TV," *Baton Rouge Morning Advocate*, 3 December 1982, p. 6-A.
70. "Swan Song for TV in Senate," *Broadcasting*, 13 December 1982, p. 35.

71. "Senate Television," *Broadcasting*, 24 January 1983, p. 38.
72. "House Outtakes of C-SPAN Complicate TV in Senate," *Broadcasting*, 14 February 1983, pp. 86–88.
73. "Trying Again to Get TV into the Senate," *Broadcasting*, 21 February 1983, p. 37.
74. "House Outtakes of C-SPAN," pp. 86–88. See also, "C-SPAN Outtakes Used as Campaign Ammunition," pp. 50–51.
75. *Congressional Record* 129 (daily ed., 16 February 1983)S1239–40.
76. "Trying Again to Get TV into the Senate," p. 37.

7. THE IMPACT OF CONGRESSIONAL TELEVISION

1. Denis S. Rutkus, "Television Network News Coverage of Senate Committees," in Senate Temporary Select Committee to Study the Senate Committee System, *Operation of the Senate Committee System: Staffing, Scheduling, Communications, Procedures, and Special Functions*, 95th Cong., 1st sess., 1977, Appendix to the Second Report, pp. 108–9.
2. Jeanette Smyth, "TV Lights, Invitations, Kisses and Phone Calls," *Washington Post*, 18 July 1973, p. B1+.
3. David Halberstam, *The Powers That Be* (New York: Alfred A. Knopf, 1979), pp. 695–97.
4. Kurt Lang and Gladys Engel Lang, "Televised Hearings: The Impact Out There," *Columbia Journalism Review*, 12(November/December 1973):52.
5. David L. Paletz, "Television Drama: The Appeals of the Senate Watergate Hearings," *The Midwest Quarterly*, 18(October 1976):105–8.
6. Lang and Lang, "Televised Hearings," pp. 52–53.
7. See Chapter 4. Additional data on audience size and demographics for the Watergate hearings are provided in C. Edward Wotring, David J. LeRoy and Gregg Phifer, "Watergate: Who's Watching the Hearings," *Public Telecommunications Review*, 1(August 1973):5–11; and C. Edward Wotring and David J. LeRoy, "The Decline of the Watergate Audience," *Public Telecommunications Review*, 2(February 1974):28–33.
8. David H. Weaver, Maxwell E. McCombs, Charles Spellman, "Watergate and the Media: A Case Study of Agenda-Setting," *American Politics Quarterly*, 3(October 1975):458–72.
9. Lang and Lang, "Televised Hearings," p. 54.

10. Joseph T. Klapper, *The Effects of Mass Communication* (New York: The Free Press, 1960), p. 5.

11. Lang and Lang, "Televised Hearings," pp. 54–57. See also, Garrett J. O'Keefe, Jr. and Harold Mendelsohn, "Voter Selectivity, Partisanship, and the Challenge of Watergate"; John Holm, Sidney Kraus and Arthur P. Bochner, "Communication and Opinion Formation"; John P. Robinson, "Public Opinion During the Watergate Crisis"; David J. LeRoy, E. Edward Wotring and Jack Lyle, "The Public Television Viewer and the Watergate Hearings"; and Alex S. Edelstein and Diane P. Tefft, "Media Credibility and Respondent Credulity with Respect to Watergate," all in *Communications Research*, 1(October 1974):345–439.

12. See Jack Dennis and Carol Webster, "Children's Images of the President and of Government in 1962 and 1974"; Robert Parker Hawkins, Suzanne Pingree and Donald F. Roberts, "Watergate and Political Socialization"; and Harrell R. Rodgers, Jr. and Edward B. Lewis, "Student Attitudes Toward Mr. Nixon," all in *American Politics Quarterly*, 3(October 1975):386–436.

13. Michael J. Robinson, "A Twentieth-Century Medium in a Nineteenth-Century Legislature: The Effects of Television on the American Congress," in *Congress in Change*, ed. Norman J. Ornstein (New York: Praeger Publishers, 1975), pp. 241–45.

14. Robinson, "A Twentieth-Century Medium," p. 252. Closely associated with Robinson's "Second Law" is the principle enunciated several years ago by communication theorists that "mass media are themselves widely regarded with awe and apparently confer status on the persons and concepts for which they are vehicles." Klapper, *The Effects of Mass Communication*, p. 129.

15. Marjorie Hunter, "On Need for the Senate To Enter the TV Age," *New York Times*, 31 October 1981, p. 11.

16. Steve Rutkus, "How Televised Floor Proceedings Might Affect the House," in House Committee on Rules, *Broadcasting the Proceedings of the House*, 95th Cong., 2d sess., 1978, H. Rept. 95–881, pp. 46–49.

17. Warren Weaver, *Both Your Houses* (New York: Praeger Publishers, 1972), p. 17.

18. Bill Roeder, "The Stage-Struck Solons," *Newsweek*, 21 May 1979, p. 23.

19. "Members Grandstanding, O'Neill Charges, Proposes Curbing House TV Show," *Cleveland Plain Dealer*, 4 August 1979, p. 4-A.

20. "O'Neill Backs Down on Threat to TV System," *Broadcasting*, 10 September 1979, p. 34.

21. Rutkus, "How Televised Floor Proceedings Might Affect the House," p. 46.
22. Ibid.
23. Ibid.
24. Ibid., p. 50.
25. W. Henson Moore, Member, U.S. House of Representatives, interview with author, Washington, D.C., 15 May 1979.
26. Rutkus, "How Televised Floor Proceedings Might Affect the House," p. 46.
27. "Sales of House Tapes Lag," Columbus (Ohio) Dispatch, 4 June 1979, p. A–7.
28. Rutkus, "How Televised Floor Proceedings Might Affect the House," p. 46.
29. Warren Weaver, Jr., "Television Adds Twist to Morning Ritual," New York Times, 26 November 1981, sec. B, p. 8.
30. House of Representatives, Viewers' Guide to the Televised Proceedings of the U.S. House of Representatives (Washington, D.C.: Government Printing Office, 1980), p. 54.
31. Roger H. Davidson and Walter J. Oleszek, Congress and Its Members (Washington, D.C.: Congressional Quarterly Press, 1981), p. 138.
32. Irwin Arieff, "House TV Gets Mixed Reviews But Cancellation Isn't Likely," Congressional Quarterly, 15 March 1980, pp. 735–36.
33. Irwin Arieff, "Move Fails to Put a Damper on Congress' 'Happy Hour,' " Congressional Quarterly, 2 August 1980, p. 2191.
34. "O'Neill Likes Televised House," Baton Rouge Morning Advocate, 8 February 1982, p. 3-A.
35. Michael J. Robinson, "Three Faces of Congressional Media," in The New Congress, eds. Thomas E. Mann and Norman J. Ornstein (Washington, D.C.: American Enterprise Institute for Public Policy Research, 1981), p. 68.
36. Senate Committee on Rules and Administration, Television and Radio Coverage of Proceedings in the Senate Chamber, 97th Cong., 1st sess., 1981, Hearings, p. 190.
37. "Cable Stats," CableVision, 7 March 1983, p. 175.
38. "Congress Watchers," Broadcasting, 7 June 1982, p. 10.
39. "Cable Stats," p. 175.
40. Gary Rothbart, "C-SPAN Troubles," CableVision, 19 April 1982, p. 23.
41. Lloyd Grove, "Television Cameras Awaiting Senate's Advice and Consent," Cleveland Plain Dealer, 26 July 1981, p. 9-D.
42. "O'Neill Backs Down on Threat to TV System," p. 34.

43. Lewis A. Froman, *The Congressional Process* (Boston: Little, Brown, 1967), p. 66.
44. Christopher H. Sterling and Timothy R. Haight, *The Mass Media: Aspen Institute Guide to Communication Industry Trends* (New York: Praeger Publishers, 1978), p. 375.
45. Mark R. Levy, "The Audience for Television News Interview Programs," *Journal of Broadcasting*, 22(Summer 1978):340–44.
46. Ibid., p. 343.
47. James N. Rosenau, *Citizenship Between Elections* (New York: The Free Press, 1974), pp. 90–92.
48. Ibid., p. 103.
49. Ibid., pp. 257–61.
50. Ibid., pp. 291–93.
51. Ibid., p. 300.
52. Ibid., pp. 304–6.
53. Sidney Verba and Norman H. Nie, *Participation in America* (New York: Harper & Row, Publishers, 1972), pp. 125–26.
54. Rosenau, *Citizenship Between Elections*, p. 4.
55. Roger H. Davidson and Glenn R. Parker, "Positive Support for Political Institutions: The Case of Congress," *The Western Political Quarterly*, 25(December 1972):604–5.
56. Douglas Cater, *Power in Washington*, special ed. (New York: Random House, 1975), pp. 125–26.
57. Clem Miller, *Member of the House*, ed. John W. Baker (New York: Charles Scribner's Sons, 1962), p. 4. See also Richard Bolling, *House Out of Order* (New York: E.P. Dutton & Co., 1965), pp. 17–19.
58. Henry Z. Schelle, "Some Reactions by Congressmen to Speaking in the U.S. House of Representatives," *Today's Speech*, 14(February 1966):20.
59. James A. Robinson, "The Role of the Rules Committee in Arranging the Program of the U.S. House of Representatives," *The Western Political Quarterly*, 12(September 1959):653.
60. Schelle, "Some Reactions by Congressmen," p. 19.
61. Donald G. Tacheron and Morris K. Udall, *The Job of the Congressman*, 2d ed. (Indianapolis, Ind.: The Bobbs-Merrill Co., Inc., 1970), pp. 211–12.
62. Ibid., pp. 254–55. The first three sources are found collectively in *Rules of the House of Representatives* and the last is found in *Deschler's Precedents of the United States House of Representatives*. Both are updated and reissued under new document numbers during each Congress.

63. See, for instance, Walter J. Oleszek, *Congressional Procedures and the Policy Process* (Washington, D.C.: Congressional Quarterly Press, 1978), pp. 105–31; Froman, *The Congressional Process*, pp. 62–99; and Tacheron and Udall, *The Job of the Congressman*, pp. 253–87.

64. Tacheron and Udall, *The Job of the Congressman*, pp. 204–5.

65. Sidney Kraus, "Mass Communication and Political Socialization: A Re-Assessment of Two Decades of Research," *Quarterly Journal of Speech*, 59(December 1973):392.

66. Robert Weissberg, *Political Learning, Political Choice, and Democratic Citizenship* (Englewood Cliffs, N.J.: Prentice-Hall, Inc., 1974), p. 43.

67. Ibid., p. 143.

68. Kraus, "Mass Communication and Political Socialization," pp. 398–400.

69. V. O. Key, Jr., *Public Opinion and American Democracy*, (New York: Alfred A. Knopf, 1967), pp. 301–2.

70. Fred Wood, Vary T. Coates, Robert Chartrand, and Richard F. Ericson, "Videoconferencing Via Satellite: Opening Congress to the People," The George Washington University Program of Policy Studies in Science and Technology, Experiment 25, April 1979, Final Report, pp. 1–41.

71. Ibid., pp. 42–50.

72. Frederick Williams, *The Communications Revolution* (Beverly Hills, Calif.: Sage Publications, 1982), p. 198.

Bibliographical Essay

The major portion of this study is based upon congressional documents. Although these documents generally carry the imprint of specific committees and subcommittees, special note must be made of the important contributions of the Congressional Research Service (CRS) in preparing many of them. One CRS study, *Congress and Mass Communications: An Institutional Perspective* (prepared for the Joint Committee on Congressional Operations, 93rd Cong., 2d sess., 1974) was instrumental in serving not only as a basis for this book, but also as the origin of the author's interest in the entire subject of congressional television.

The story of radio's early years and of the role the military played in developing the U.S. broadcasting industry is superbly documented in L. S. Howeth's *History of Communications-Electronics in the United States Navy* (Washington, D.C.: Government Printing Office, 1963). Gleason Archer provides a more comprehensive examination of radio's formative years in his *History of Radio to 1926* (New York: The American Historical Society, Inc., 1938) but omits many of the military details that Howeth includes. For all the information that Howeth and Archer provide, both give only scant attention to congressional use of radio. The *Congressional Record* fills in many of the holes, as does the somewhat opinionated periodical *Radio Broadcast*. However, the best source of information on congressional radio during the 1930s and 1940s is Robert E. Summers' doctoral dissertation, "The Role of Congressional Broadcasting in a Democratic Society" (The Ohio State University, 1955). Summers expands his chronological account of congressional radio development into an enlightening philosophical treatise on a democratic government's information responsibilities.

The Summers dissertation also carries the reader through the transition from congressional radio to congressional television. Again, the *Congressional Record* is an obviously unsurpassed resource document with its reporting of floor debate on congressional television matters, particularly during the 1970s and 1980s.

The early 1950s were years of intense interest in televised congressional hearings both for their subjects and for what critics claimed was television's powerful impact on the hearing process itself. Critical commentary is confined primarily to law review articles such as those found in the *Journal of the Federal Communications Bar Association* (later renamed the *Federal Communications Bar Journal* and now called the *Federal Communications Law Journal*), although there are some books like Edward Bennett Williams's *One Man's Freedom* (New York: Atheneum, 1962) that devote several pages to discussing the subject. The *New York Times*, *Washington Post* and *Broadcasting/Telecasting* (now *Broadcasting*) magazine also provide daily accounts of television's hearing coverage as well as editorials and special columns on the subject. *Broadcasting* magazine's special interest reporting on this topic and on later efforts toward implementing television coverage of the House and Senate is noteworthy. The publication is as much a chronicle of the broadcasting industry's side of the congressional television story as the *Congressional Record* is for that of Congress. And not to be overlooked is the *Congressional Quarterly*, whose coverage of Congress's weekly activities has yielded some especially good congressional television articles, particularly those by writers Ann Cooper and Irwin Arieff.

Various documents resulting from the activity of the Joint Committee on the Organization of the Congress trace the progress of what eventually became the 1970 Legislative Reorganization Act. *On Capitol Hill*, 2nd ed. (Hinsdale, Ill.: Dryden Press, 1972) is a scholarly account of the Joint Committee's activity written by John F. Bibby and Roger H. Davidson. The authors' academic perspective affords the reader a view of the "why" and "how" for certain provisions of the 1970 Reorganization Act—the law that would provide the basis for the House decision almost a decade later to allow telecasts of its chamber proceedings.

The power struggle between the President and Congress to attract media coverage, especially that of television, is the subject of *Presidential Television* by Newton Minow, John B. Martin, and Lee M. Mitchell (New York: Basic Books, 1973). So effective was President Nixon's frequent use of television for addressing viewers on the Vietnam War that

Bibliographical Essay 185

several in Congress attempted to secure a comparable direct congressional access to the medium. The story of this ill-fated venture is best told in the Senate Communications Subcommittee's hearing transcript, *Public Service Time for the Legislative Branch* (91st Cong., 2d sess., 1970).

Watergate presented television with a tremendous public service opportunity. How the medium responded is detailed in *Watergate: Chronology of a Crisis* (Washington, D.C.: Congressional Quarterly, Inc., 1975). This publication is unsurpassed in its daily account of the tangled web of events that were a part of Watergate. James Hamilton examines some of the legal issues of the Ervin Committee's Watergate hearings in *The Power to Probe* (New York: Random House, 1976). Hamilton makes some especially insightful comments on the legal issues of television's role in the Ervin Committee hearings.

Although much of the literature that is available on congressional television during the 1970s and early 1980s is found in government documents (with the exception of the continued reporting in the above mentioned newspapers and periodicals), two non-congressional publications are particularly noteworthy. The first is *Congress and the News Media* (New York: Hastings House, 1974), a book edited by Robert Blanchard that is packed with informative articles on press coverage of Congress. The second is a booklet distributed by the Twentieth Century Fund Task Force on Broadcasting and the Legislature entitled *Openly Arrived At* (New York: The Twentieth Century Fund, 1974). *Openly Arrived At* examines the pros and cons of televising House and Senate sessions, chronicles the information needs and responsibilities of Congress, and briefly summarizes the uses made of television by several state legislatures and foreign parliaments.

The Joint Committee on Congressional Operations initiated the efforts that would result in House chamber television. A series of documents details not only the committee's activities but also practically every facet of television's role (or probable role) in covering legislative proceedings. The document series begins with committee hearings entitled *Congress and Mass Communications* (93rd Cong., 2d sess., 1974) and concludes with two reports issued simultaneously by the House and Senate. The first is *Broadcasting House and Senate Proceedings* (93rd Cong., 2d sess., 1974, S. Rept. 93–1275), and the second is *A Clear Message to the People* (94th Cong., 1st sess., 1975, S. Rept. 94–419).

Additional hearings were conducted by both the House Ad Hoc Subcommittee on Broadcasting and the full House Rules Committee and issued under the title *Television and Radio Coverage of the House* (94th Cong., 1st sess., 1975, and 2d sess., 1976). Four committee prints were issued by the same subcommittee during 1975 and 1976, all under the general title of *Broadcast Coverage of House Floor Proceedings* and all serving as explanations of various resolutions introduced by House members to implement some form of House television. The number (a total of four) and content of these prints denote the controversy surrounding the question of who would finally control a House television system if indeed it did become a reality.

The House's move toward opening its legislative chamber to television was well underway by 1977. All that remained was fine tuning implementation procedures, defining rules, and purchasing the equipment. The manner in which the House attended to these details is provided in the Select (formerly the Joint) Committee on Congressional Operations, *Televising the House* (95th Cong., 1st sess., 1977, H. Doc. 95-231) and the House Committee on Rules, *Broadcasting the Proceedings of the House* (95th Cong., 2d sess., 1978, H. Rept. 95-881).

The Senate has yet to follow the House's television example, but it has given some serious thought to the possibility. The findings of the Joint Committee on Congressional Operations had just as much application to Senate chamber television as to House chamber television, though the Senate obviously was much less impressed by the committee's contributions. Nonetheless, the Commission on the Operation of the Senate issued a compilation of papers in 1977 entitled *Senate Communications with the Public* (94th Cong., 2d sess., 1977) in which several authors suggested that the Senate might improve its image by televising its chamber proceedings; in particular, Len Allen's paper, "Television from the Senate Floor," deserves special attention for the author's efforts in building a case for television's positive impact on Senate floor activity.

The Senate Committee on Rules and Administration's careful examination of Senate television needs and, more important, of Senate receptiveness to chamber television is contained in the committee's hearings *Television and Radio Coverage of Proceedings in the Senate Chamber* (97th Cong., 1st sess., 1981). What appeared to be the document that would establish final rules for Senate chamber television, the same committee's *Regulations to Implement Television and Radio Coverage of Senate Proceedings* (97th Cong., 2d sess., 1982, S. Rept. 97-506), makes for interesting reading but, as of this writing, has yet to serve its intended purpose.

Index

ABC (American Broadcasting Company), 38, 46, 47, 64, 89, 110
Academy of Television Arts and Sciences, 38
Access time. See Public service time
Actuality, 8
Adams, William C., 12
Ad Hoc Subcommittee on Broadcasting, 88-94
Agenda-setting, 134
Albert, Carl, 90-91, 92, 93, 94
Allen, Len, 86-87
American Bar Association, 75
American Broadcasting Company. See ABC
American Civil Liberties Union, 49
American Federation of Labor, 30
Anderson, John, 75; and abuse of House recordings, 113-114, 117; advocates implementing House television, 87, 88, 92, 93; criticizes House television test, 97-98; and House television management system, 102, 104-105, 110-111
Anderson Resolution, 102

Appel, Kevin, 12
AP (Associated Press) Radio, 110
Architect of the Capitol, 98; and Senate television, 121-122, 127
Army-McCarthy hearings, 46-47, 49, 133
Associated Press (AP) Radio, 110
Attentive public, 146-148

Bach, Stanley, 121
Badillo, Herman, 75
Baker, Howard, 70, 118-119, 137; proposes Senate television, 119-120, 123, 124, 125, 127-128
Blanchard, Robert, 11, 12
Bolling, Richard, 60
Brennan, Vincent, 25-26
Broadcast Advisory Board, 90, 91
Broadcast Advisory Committee, 114-115
Broadcasting Magazine, 68, 104
Brooks, Jack, 79, 87, 89, 90, 114
Brooks plan (H. Res 269) for House television, 87, 89, 90
Budget, fiscal 1980, 138

Byrd, Robert, 83-84, 86, 95, 96; and Senate television, 118, 125, 126

Cable Satellite Public Affairs Network, 116, 117, 118, 122, 143
Cable television, 81, 108-109, 116, 122, 142-143
Cain, Harry, 39
Canadian House of Commons, 107, 108-109, 115
Cannon, Howard, 126
Capitol Hill press corps, 9. *See also* Congressional correspondent
Cater, Douglas, 13
CBS (Columbia Broadcasting System), 46-47, 64, 66, 89, 96, 110
Chambers, Whittaker, 36-37
Clawson, Delwin, 88
Clerk of the U.S. House, 91, 117
Closed-circuit television, 58, 82, 85, 109, 113
Cloture motion, 124
Coalition for Professional Broadcast Coverage of House Floor, 109
Code of conduct, for congressional hearings, 41, 47-50. *See also* Committee code of fair practices
Coelho, Tony, 118
Coffee, John, 30-31, 32-33
Columbia Broadcasting System. *See* CBS
Commerical sponsorship, of House telecasts, 89
Commission on the Operation of the Senate, 86-87
Committee code of fair practice, 47, 49, 62-63
Committee hearings. *See* Congressional committee hearings; *names of individual committees*
Committee for the Re-election of the President, 71

Communications Act of 1934, 18, 65, 68, 159n. 84
Communications satellite, 81, 108-109, 152
Congress: public attitudes toward and public confidence in, 3-6; public knowledge of activity, 6-7
Congressional access time, to television, 63-64, 65-69
Congressional committee hearings: broadcast vs. print media coverage, 43; code of fair practices, 41, 47-50; debate over television coverage role, 38-46, 47-50; effects of televised, on participants and viewers, 131-135, 164n. 47; function, 35-36; as grand jury, 45-46; interruption of, blamed on camera crews, 165n. 49; origins of telecasts, 36-37; and the President, 14; procedural rules, 48; publicity value of telecasts, 13-15; telecast of House, 50-54; telecast of Senate, 37-50; and television, 35, 36-54; and television news, 14-15. See also *names of individual committees*
Congressional committee investigative hearings. *See* Congressional committee hearings
Congressional correspondent, 11. *See also* Capitol Hill press corps
Congressional hearings. *See* Congressional committee hearings
Congressional investigative hearings. *See* Congressional committee hearings
Congressional meetings, 13
Congressional policy-making, 20-23
Congressional-presidential relationship, 20-22
Congressional Record, 115, 138, 139-140, 149

Index

Congressional reform, 20-23, 57-63
Congressional reorganization. *See* Congressional reform
Congressional Research Service (CRS), 7, 19, 77-78, 121, 137-140
Congressional right of television access, 63-64, 65-69
Congressmen: contact with the press, 9; public attitudes toward, 3-5; and recording facilities, 8-9; reliance on television news for publicity, 7-9
Congress of Industrial Organizations, 30
Connecticut Educational Television Corporation, 80
Connecticut legislature, 80
Control system, for House television. *See* House television, management system
Copyright, of House recordings, 90
Cox, Archibald, 72-73
CRS. *See* Congressional Research Service
C-SPAN. *See* Cable-Satellite Public Affairs Network

Dean, John, 71, 73
Debate. *See* House chamber debate
Democratic Congressional Campaign Committee, 118
Dennis, David, 63
Derwinski, Edward, 117
Detroit Common Council, 51
Dill, Clarence, 28
Dirksen, Everett, 31-32
Dole, Robert, 72
Domenici, Peter, 128
Drinan, Robert, 75
Due process: and congressional committee hearings telecasts, 43; and Watergate hearings telecast, 72-74

Dumont television network, 38, 46
Durkin, John, 85

Edmondson, Ed, 58
Equal opportunity, Communications Act provisions, 18, 68, 159n. 84
Equal time. *See* equal opportunity
Ervin, Sam, 70, 73, 132
Ervin Committee, 70-74, 132. *See also* Senate Watergate hearings
Executive Committee of the Radio Correspondents' Galleries of the U.S. Capitol, 51
Executive department documents, 149
Extended hearing, as argument for televising congressional committee hearings, 42

Fairness Doctrine, 65, 68, 69
Federal Communications Commission, 18, 65
Fenno, Richard, 4-5
Ferber, Paul H., 12
Florida legislature, 80
Ford, Gerald, 18, 19-20
Ford, Wendell, 122, 125-126
Formal presidential address, 18-20, 64, 65
Friendly, Fred, 66, 80
Fulbright, William, 65-69

Galloway, George, 41
Gallup poll, 71, 76, 134
Gavel to Gavel: A Guide to the Televised Proceedings of Congress, 151
George Washington University Program of Policy Studies in Science and Technology, 152
Goldenson, Leonard, 68
Goldman, Ralph, 35
Goodman, Julian, 20
Gore, Albert, 115-116

Grandstanding, as a result of House television, 137-138
"Great debates," telecast from Senate chamber, 58
Green, June, 73
Gurney, Edward, 70

Halberstam, David, 66, 132
Harbord, James G., 26
Harding, Warren G., 26
Harris, Oren, 53
Hatfield, Mark, 64, 65
Hearing transcripts, 149
"Herd" journalism, 11
Hiss, Alger, 36-37
Hiss-Chambers hearings, 36-37
Hopkins, Bruce R., 23
House Administration Committee, 141-142
House chamber debate: procedure and assignments, 150; role in legislative process, 149-150; television effects on prolonging, 138
House chamber proceedings: criticism, 148-149; rules, 150-151; and television viewer information, 149-151
House Commerce Subcommittee on Communications, 118
House Commission on Administrative Review, 3-4, 5, 6, 7
House Commission on Information and Facilities, 89
House committee telecasts, 36-37, 41, 50-54, 62-63; procedural rules, 62
House Judiciary Committee, 74-76
House Recording Studio, 8-9, 98
House "Recording Studio Rate Schedule," 8-9
House of Representatives: effects of television on proceedings, 136-142; proposals for televising chamber proceedings, 87-94; recording of proceedings, 116-118; telecast of proceedings implemented, 113-116
House Rules Committee, 62, 88, 90, 91, 92, 93; hearings on House television management system, 101-103; recommendations for House television management system, 105-109
House Rules Committee Ad Hoc Subcommittee on Broadcasting, 88-94
House Rules Committee Subcommittee on the Rules and Organization of the House, 103-104
House television: effects on House membership and proceedings, 136-142; effects on viewers, 142-151; implementation efforts, 97-112; implementation rules, 113; management system, 102, 103, 104, 105-107, 109, 110-112
House Un-American Activities Committee, 36-37, 41, 50-51
Howell, Robert, 26, 27, 28
Hughes, Harold, 86

Impeachment proceedings, 74-76
Inouye, Daniel, 70, 126
Interactive video, 151-152
Interview programs, 12, 145-146
Investigations Subcommittee of the Senate Committee on Expenditures in the Executive Department, 49
Investigative committee hearings. See Congressional committee hearings

Javits, Jacob, 58
Jerome, James, 107, 108
Johnson, Lyndon, 64
Joint Committee on Congressional Operations, 59, 63, 87; conducts

Index   191

Congress and mass communication hearings, 76-77, 79-81, 82-83
Joint Committee on the Organization of Congress (1945), 31-33, 57
Joint Committee on the Organization of Congress (1966), 20-21, 57-60, 63
Jordan, Frank, 60
Judiciary Committee. *See* House Judiciary Committee

Katyn Forest massacre, 50
Kefauver, Estes, 32, 37-38, 48
Kefauver Committee, 37-38
Kefauver Committee hearings, 37-38; and code of fair practices, 48-49; debate over role of television coverage, 38-46; effects on viewers, 133
Klapper, Joseph, 135
Kleinman, Morris, 38-40, 44-45
Kleinman-Rothkopf decision, 44-45
Koch, Edward, 5
Korff, Baruch, 73
Kraus, Sidney, 151
Kurland, Philip B., 69

LaFollette, Robert M., 31
LaFollette-Monroney Committee, 31-33, 57
Lamb, Brian, 117, 118, 143
Lang, Gladys Engel, 132, 134
Lang, Kurt, 132, 134
Latta, Delbert, 60
"Law of Videopolitics," 136
Leamer, Lawrence, 14
Legislative process, 149-150
Legislative Reorganization Act of 1946, 22, 33
Legislative Reorganization Act of 1970, 22-23, 63
Levy, Mark R., 145-146
Library of Congress, 89-90, 127
Long, Gillis, 101, 103, 111, 112, 114

Long, Russell, 119, 120, 123, 124, 125, 128
Lucas, Scott W., 36, 41, 47-48
Lynch, John, 60, 61

McCarthy, Joseph, 46, 47, 133
McClure, James, 85, 86
McClure Resolution, 85-86
McCormack, John, 53-54
McGovern, George, 64, 65
McGovern-Hatfield Amendment, 64
Madden, Ray, 58, 92, 94
Magruder, Jeb, 73
Management system, for House television. *See* House television, management system
Mansfield, Mike, 70, 85, 86
Martin, Joseph, 51, 52
Mass media, and status conferral, 179n. 14
Master Antenna Television System, 98
Mathias, Charles, 119, 127, 128-129
Matsunaga, Spark, 96
Meader, George, 51, 52, 53, 58
Metcalf, Lee, 76-77, 79, 83
Michel, Robert, 117
Military Procurement Authorization Act, 64
Mitchell, Lee M., 11, 15
Monroney, Mike, 31, 57, 58
Montoya, Joseph, 70
Morning hour, and House proceedings, 140-141
Mudd, Roger, 60, 61
Murphy, Morgan, 88
Murrow, Edward R., 47
Muskie, Edmund, 79
Mutual Broadcasting System, 110

Narrowcasting, 81
National Archives, 127

National Assessment of Educational Progress, 6
National Association of Broadcasters (NAB), 109
National Association of Radio-Television Broadcasters, 52
National Broadcasting Company. *See* NBC
National Commission on the Reform of Secondary Education, 6
National News Council, 109
National Planning Association, 30
National Public Radio (NPR), 95-96, 110
National Task Force on Citizenship Education, 6
Navy Department, 26, 27
NBC (National Broadcasting Company), 46, 47, 64, 89, 96, 110
Network plan, for House television, 89, 90
Network pool arrangement, for televising House proceedings, 91, 93-94
Network pool system, for managing House television, 106, 107
New York State Bar Association, 49
New York Times, 76, 104
Nie, Norman H., 147
Ninety-day House television test, 97-101; evaluation of, 98, 99-100, 102-103
Nixon, Richard, 64, 65, 74-76, 135
NPR. *See* National Public Radio
Nye, Gerald, 28

O'Conor, Herbert, 39-40
O'Neil, Thomas, 91, 92, 97, 98, 103, 104; and House television implementation, 109-110, 112; on House television impact, 138, 141

One-minute speeches, and House proceedings, 121, 140
Open meeting (sunshine) rules, 22
Opinion survey, 3-7; and Army-McCarthy hearings, 47; and House committee hearings telecasts, 58; and House Judiciary Committee impeachment proceedings telecast, 76; and House television management system, 93; and radio coverage of congressional proceedings, 30; and radio coverage of Panama Canal Treaty Senate debate, 96; and Senate chamber proceedings telecast, 119; and television effects on House chamber proceedings, 141-142; and Watergate awareness, 134; and Watergate hearing telecasts, 71, 72
Owens, Wayne, 75

Panama Canal Treaty, 94-97
Panama Canal Treaty Debate, 95-97, 122
Parliamentary procedure, 150-151
Parliamentary radio, 27-28
PBS. *See* Public Broadcasting Service
Pell, Claiborne, 126
Pepper, Claude, 30-31, 32, 88, 93
Permanent Investigations Subcommittee, 46. *See also* Army-McCarthy hearings
Phenomenistic theory, 135
Pierson, Theodore, 68
Pittman, Key, 28
Political campaign, prohibition of House television recordings for, 89
Political participation, and House television viewership, 146-148
Political socialization: and television, 151; and Watergate hearings, 135

Index

Polling, 152
Polls. See Opinion survey
Polsby, Nelson, 13
Presidency, Watergate-induced perceptions of, 135
President, 14; role in congressional policy-making, 21-22; television coverage, 15-20
Presidential address, 18-20, 64, 65
Presidential impeachment, 74-76
Presidential press conference, 17-18, 64
Press, 9-11
Press conference, 17-18, 64
Press gallery, 9-10, 83
Pressler, Larry, 123-124
Press release, 8, 9
Public Broadcasting Service (PBS), 76, 89, 94. See also Public television
Public education, as a function of House television, 148-149
Public information, as a function of House television, 148-149
Publicity: presidential dominance of, 16; reliance of individual congressmen on television for, 7-9; value of congressional committees for, 13-14
Public service time, for congressional television access, 65-69
Public television, 71. See also Public Broadcasting Service

Radio, 25, 28-29; attitudes toward congressional, 29, 30; legislation pertaining to implementation of congressional, 25-27, 28, 30-31; Senate Panama Canal Treaty debate coverage, 95-97; and Senate proceedings coverage, 122
Radio and Television Correspondents' Galleries, Executive Committee, 9

Radio and Television Galleries, 9-11
Radio Broadcast, 27
Radio networks, and congressional speaking policies, 29
Radio-Television Correspondents' Association, 52
Radio-Television News Directors Association, 109
Radio-television reporters, 9-11
Rayburn, Sam, 34; bans House committee television, 50-54, 62
Rebman, Fred, 80
Recording facilities. See House Recording Studio; Senate Recording Studio
Recordings, of House proceedings, 116-118
Reform. See Congressional reform
Reorganization. See Congressional reform
Reporters, 9-11
Republican Congressional Committee, 118
Right of access. See Public service time
"Right of privacy," and congressional committee hearing telecasts, 44
"Right to know," as argument for televising congressional committee hearings, 42-43
Roberts, Bill, 60
Robinson, Michael J., 9, 12, 136, 141
Rockefeller, Nelson, 83
Rose, Charlie, 114-115, 117-118
Rosenau, James N., 146, 147
Rothkopf, Louis, 38-40, 44-45
Rovere, Richard, 42-43
Ryan, Leo, 103

Saeman, John, 122
SALT debate, 118-119
School systems, and House television viewing, 144

Schweinhaut, Henry, 44-45
Scott, Hugh, 85
Select Committee on Congressional Operations, 98, 100-101. *See also* Joint Committee on Congressional Operations
Senate, 12-13, 83-84, 85-86; and television coverage of proceedings, 118-129
Senate Amendment to End the War, 64-65
Senate Armed Services Committee, 36
Senate Commerce Committee Communications Subcommittee, 66-68
Senate Committee on Expenditures in the Executive Departments, 48
Senate Committee on Government Operations, 46
Senate Foreign Relations Committee, 66
Senate Recording Studio, 8-9, 127
Senate Rules and Administration Committee, 95, 119; examines Senate television, 119-120, 121-123, 125-127, 129
Senate Select Committee on Presidential Campaign Activities. *See* Ervin Committee
Senate Sergeant of Arms, 122-123, 127
Senate Subcommittee on Intergovernmental Relations, 4, 5, 6-7, 77, 79
Senate television: coverage of chamber proceedings, 118-129; effects on Senate procedure, 121; technical requirements, 121-122
Senate Watergate hearings, 70-74; viewer impact, 132, 133, 134, 135
"Sense of the House," as House television resolution terminology, 94
Separation of powers doctrine, 45, 73

Sheehan, William, 20
Sirica, John, 73
Sisk, B. F., 60, 103, 104, 105; chairs Ad Hoc Subcommittee on Broadcasting, 88, 92, 93
Sisk Subcommittee, 88-94
Small, Bill, 60
Smith, H. Allen, 60
Snee, Joseph M., 44
Society of Professional Journalists, 109
Speaker of the House, control of House floor activity, 91
Speaker's Broadcast Advisory Committee, 114-115
Special order speeches, 121, 140-141
Special Senate Committee to Investigate Organized Crime in Interstate Commerce. *See* Kefauver Committee
Special Subcommittee on Legislative Reorganization, 60-62
Stanton, Frank, 67
Stennis, John, 123
Stephens, G. Douglas, 117
Stockman, David, 114
Strategic Arms Limitation Treaty. *See* SALT debate
Study Group on Senate Practices and Procedures, 126
Summers, Robert E., 33, 55
Sundquist, James L., 21
Sunshine (open meeting), 13; rules, 22

Talmadge, Herman, 70
Taylor, Telford, 45
Technological revolution, and congressional communication, 152-153
Television access, for congressmen, 63-69
Television feasibility study, and the House, 89

Index   195

Television from the Senate Floor, 86-87
Television interview, 8
Television interview programs, 12, 145-146
Television news: concentration on the President, 17; coverage of congressional activity, 5-15; and House one-minute speeches, 121
Television viewers: impact of televised congressional committee hearings, 132-135; impact of televised House proceedings, 142-151
Time cues, and the *Congressional Record*, 115

Unanimous consent, and Senate television debate, 86
Union contracts, and House television, 101-102
Union for Democratic Action, 30
United Nations, 82
United Press International Audio, 110
United States v. Kleinman et al., 164nn. 46, 47
United States v. Orman, 164n. 47
Unlimited debate, and Senate television, 86
UPI Audio, 110
U.S. House of Representatives. *See* House of Representatives
U.S. Senate. *See* Senate
U.S. v. Moran, 164n. 47

Van Deerlin, Lionel, 118
Vander Jagt, Guy, 118
Van Dyke, Charles, 110
Verba, Sidney, 147
Videoconferences, 152
Videotape recordings, 116-118
Video technology, 151-153
Vietnam War, 64-65, 66

Viewers' Guide to the Televised Proceedings of the U.S. House of Representatives, 151
Viewing audience: characteristics of, for House television, 147-148; composition and description for House television, 144-145; impact of televised congressional committee hearings, 132-135; impact of televised House proceedings, 142-151
Vivian, Weston, 58

Walter, Francis, 53
War Department, 26, 27
Warner, John, 120
Washington Post, 96, 104, 114, 116
Wasilewski, Vincent, 60-61, 68
Watergate, 23, 69-70, 134
Watergate hearings, 70-74, 132, 133, 134, 135
Weicker, Lowell, 70
Wertheimer, Linda, 96
WETA-TV, 116
Wheeling, West Virginia, 46
White, George M., 121-122
Wiebe, G. D., 133
Wiley, Alexander, 39
Williams, Edward Bennett, 42
Williams, Pat, 117
WJBK-TV, 37
WJCT-TV, 80
Wright, Jim, 111-112, 113-114, 141
Writers War Board, 30
WWJ-TV, 37
Wyman, Louis, 85
Wyman-Durkin debate, 85-86

Yarborough, Ralph, 58
Yokom, S. Anders, 80
Young, Andrew, 88
Young, John, 60, 92-93

About the Author

RONALD GARAY brings to his position as Associate Professor of Journalism at Louisiana State University six years of experience as a radio producer and reporter. His articles on telecommunications law and regulation and on the history and social effects of broadcasting have been published in the *Journal of Broadcasting* and *Journalism Quarterly*.

Augsburg College
George Sverdrup Library
Minneapolis, MN 55454